Jacob's Ladder

Reading Comprehension Program

Second Edition

Grade

3

Jacob's Ladder
Reading Comprehension Program

Second Edition

Grade 3

Contributing Editors:

Joyce VanTassel-Baska, Tamra Stambaugh,
Kimberley L. Chandler

Contributing Authors:

Heather French, Paula Ginsburgh,
Tamra Stambaugh, Joyce VanTassel-Baska

William & Mary
School of Education

CENTER FOR GIFTED EDUCATION

William & Mary
School of Education
Center for Gifted Education
P.O. Box 8795
Williamsburg, VA 23187

Edited by Lacy Compton

Cover design by Raquel Trevino and layout design by Allegra Denbo

ISBN-13: 978-1-61821-712-7

Prufrock Press Inc.
P.O. Box 8813
Waco, TX 76714-8813
Phone: (800) 998-2208
Fax: (800) 240-0333
http://www.prufrock.com

Table of Contents

Part I: Teachers' Guide to Jacob's Ladder Reading Comprehension Program

Introduction to *Jacob's Ladder, Grade 3*

Jacob's Ladder, Grade 3 (2nd ed.) is a supplemental reading program that implements targeted readings from short stories, poetry, and nonfiction sources, building on the work in the previous edition, *Jacob's Ladder, Level 1*. With this program, students engage in an inquiry process that moves from lower order to higher order thinking skills. Starting with basic literary understanding, students learn to critically analyze texts by determining implications and consequences, generalizations, main ideas, and/or creative synthesis. Suggested for students in grade 3 to enhance reading comprehension and critical thinking, *Jacob's Ladder, Grade 3* tasks are organized into four skill ladders: A–D. Each ladder focuses on a different skill. Students "climb" each ladder by answering lower level questions before moving to higher level questions or rungs at the top of each ladder. Each ladder stands alone and focuses on a separate critical thinking component in reading.

Ladder A focuses on implications and consequences. By leading students through sequencing and cause and effect activities, students learn to draw implications and consequences from readings. Ladder B focuses on making generalizations. Students first learn to provide details and examples, then move to classifying and organizing those details in order to make generalizations. Ladder C focuses on main ideas, themes, or concepts. Students begin by identifying setting and characters and then make inferences about the literary situation. Ladder D focuses on creative synthesis by leading students through paraphrasing and summarizing activities. Table 1 provides a visual representation of the four ladders and corresponding objectives for each ladder and rung.

The second editions in the *Jacob's Ladder* series consist of seven levels, divided by grade: K–1, 1–2, 3, 4, 5, 6–7, and 7–8. Most of the books contain short stories, poetry, and nonfiction selections, including biographies. Additionally, most of the pieces include at least two commensurate ladders for each selection, with a few exceptions (e.g., the K–1 poetry section and the Level 1 poetry section, which have one ladder per poem). *Jacob's Ladder, K–1* and *1–2* differ from the rest of the series in that the majority of the short stories are Caldecott Medal or Caldecott Honor picture books. Many of the stories are intended to be read aloud for the first reading. In addition, although *Jacob's Ladder, K–1* does contain poetry, it does not contain nonfiction selections.

Although grade-level distinctions have been set for each of the second editions, teachers may find that they want to vary usage beyond the recommended levels, depending on student abilities. Evidence suggests that the curriculum can be successfully implemented with gifted learners and advanced readers, as well as promising learners, at different grade levels. Thus, the levels vary and overlap to provide opportunities for teachers to select the most appropriate set of readings for meaningful differentiation for their gifted, bright, or promising learners.

Ladder A:
Focus on Implications and Consequences

The goal of Ladder A is to develop prediction and forecasting skills by encouraging students to make connections between the information provided. Starting with sequencing, students learn to recognize basic types of change that occur within a text. Through identifying cause-and-effect relationships, students then can judge the impact of certain events. Finally, through recognizing consequences and implications, students predict future events as logical and identify both short- and long-term consequences by judging probable outcomes based on data provided. The rungs are as follows:

- **Ladder A, Rung 1, Sequencing**: The lowest rung on the ladder, sequencing, requires students to organize a set of information in order, based on their reading (e.g., List the steps of a recipe in order).

TABLE 1
Goals and Objectives of Jacob's Ladder by Ladder and Rung

Ladder A	Ladder B	Ladder C	Ladder D
A3: Consequences and Implications Students will be able to predict character actions, story outcomes, and make real-world forecasts.	**B3: Generalizations** Students will be able to make general statements about a reading and/or an idea within the reading, using data to support their statements.	**C3: Main Idea, Theme, or Concept** Students will be able to identify a major idea, theme, or concept common throughout the text.	**D3: Creative Synthesis** Students will create something new using what they have learned from the reading and their synopses.
A2: Cause and Effect Students will be able to identify and predict relationships between character behavior and story events, and their effects upon other characters or events.	**B2: Classifications** Students will be able to categorize different aspects of the text or identify and sort categories from a list of topics or details.	**C2: Inference** Students will be able to use textual clues to read between the lines and make judgments about specific textual events, ideas, or character analysis.	**D2: Summarizing** Students will be able to provide a synopsis of text sections.
A1: Sequencing Students will be able to list, in order of importance or occurrence in the text, specific events or plot summaries.	**B1: Details** Students will be able to list specific details or recall facts related to the text or generate a list of ideas about a specific topic or character.	**C1: Literary Elements** Students will be able to identify and explain specific story elements, such as character, setting, or poetic device.	**D1: Paraphrasing** Students will be able to restate lines read using their own words.

- **Ladder A, Rung 2, Cause and Effect**: The middle rung, cause and effect, requires students to think about relationships and identify what causes certain effects and/or what effects were brought about because of certain causes (e.g., What causes a cake to rise in the oven? What effect does the addition of egg yolks have on a batter?).

- **Ladder A, Rung 3, Consequences and Implications**: The highest rung on Ladder A requires students to think about both short-term and long-term events that may happen as a result of an effect they have identified (e.g., What are the short-term and long-term consequences of not saving any money?). Students learn to see implications and determine consequences from text for application in the real world. An implication is a possible result of an action. A consequence is the actual result of an action.

Ladder B: Focus on Generalizations

The goal of Ladder B is to help students develop deductive reasoning skills, moving from the concrete elements in a story to abstract ideas. Students begin by learning the importance of concrete details and how they can be organized. By the top rung, students are able to make general statements spanning a topic or concept. The rungs are as follows:

- **Ladder B, Rung 1, Details**: The lowest rung on Ladder B, details, requires students to list examples or details from what they have read and/or to list examples they know from the real world or have read about (e.g., Make a list of examples of transportation. Write as many as you can think of in 2 minutes).

- **Ladder B, Rung 2, Classifications**: The middle rung of Ladder B focuses on students' ability to categorize examples and details based on characteristics (e.g., How might we categorize the modes of transportation you identified?). This activity builds students' skills in categorization and classification.

- **Ladder B, Rung 3, Generalizations**: The highest rung on Ladder B, generalizations, requires students to use the list and categories generated at Rungs 1 and 2 to develop 2–3 general statements that apply to *all* of their examples (e.g., Write three statements about transportation).

This ladder is based on the Taba Model of Concept Development. Hilda Taba's Concept Development model (Taba, 1962) involves both inductive and deductive reasoning processes.

The model includes the following steps:

1. Begin with a broad concept, such as *change, conflict,* or *system.*

2. List as many examples of the concept as possible.

3. Categorize the examples to determine connections and to organize ideas.

4. Think of nonexamples of the concept.

5. Develop generalizations about the concept. Generalizations are universal statements about the concept. They are abstract and high level in nature.

Ladder C: Focus on Main Ideas, Themes, or Concepts

The goal of Ladder C is to develop literary analysis skills based on an understanding of literary elements. After completing Ladder C, students may state the main idea, the theme, or the overarching concept of text after identifying setting, characters, and the context of the piece. The rungs are as follows:

- **Ladder C, Rung 1, Literary Elements**: While working on Rung 1, students identify and/or describe the setting or situation in which the reading occurs. This rung also requires students to develop an understanding of a given character by identifying qualities he or she possesses and comparing these qualities to other characters they have encountered in their reading (e.g., In *Goldilocks and the Three Bears*, what is the situation in which Goldilocks finds herself? What qualities do you admire in Goldilocks? What qualities do you find problematic? How is she similar to or different from other fairy tale characters you have encountered?).

- **Ladder C, Rung 2, Inference**: Inference serves as the middle rung of this ladder and requires students to think through a situation in the text and come to a conclusion based on the information and clues provided (e.g., What evidence exists that Goldilocks ate the porridge? What inferences can you make about the bear's subsequent action?).

- **Ladder C, Rung 3, Main Idea, Theme, or Concept**: As the highest rung of Ladder C, this step requires students to state the main idea, theme, or overarching concept for a reading. This exercise may ask students to explain an idea from the reading that best states what the text means (e.g., How would you rename the fairy tale? Why? What is the overall theme of *Goldilocks and the Three Bears*? Which of the following morals apply to the fairy tale? Why or why not?). This exercise also may require students to identify the overarching concept in a selection.

Ladder D: Focus on Creative Synthesis

The goal of Ladder D is to help students develop skills in creative synthesis in order to foster students' creation of new material based on information from the reading. It moves from the level of restating ideas to creating new ideas about a topic or concept. The rungs are as follows:

- **Ladder D, Rung 1, Paraphrasing**: The lowest rung on Ladder D is paraphrasing. This rung requires students to restate a short passage using their own words (e.g., Rewrite the following quotation in your own words: "But as soon as [the Lion] came near to Androcles, he recognized his friend, and fawned upon him, and licked his hands like a friendly dog. The emperor, surprised at this, summoned Androcles to him, who told the whole story. Whereupon the slave was pardoned and freed, and the Lion let loose to his native forest.").

- **Ladder D, Rung 2, Summarizing**: Summarizing, the middle rung, requires students to summarize larger sections of text by selecting the most important key points within a passage (e.g., Choose one section of the story and summarize it in five sentences).

- **Ladder D, Rung 3, Creative Synthesis**: The highest rung on Ladder D requires students to create something new using what they have learned from the reading and their synopses of it (e.g., Write another fable about the main idea you identified for this fable, using characters, setting, and a plot of your choice).

Process Skills

Along with the four goals addressed by the ladders, a fifth goal, process skills, is incorporated in the *Jacob's Ladder* curriculum. The aim of this goal is to promote learning through interaction and discussion of reading material in the classroom. After completing the ladders and following guidelines for discussion and teacher feedback, students will be able to:

- articulate their understanding of a reading passage using textual support,
- engage in proper dialogue about the meaning of a selection, and
- discuss varied ideas about intention of a passage both orally and in writing.

Reading Genres and Selections

The reading selections include three major genres: short stories (fables, myths, short stories, and essays), poetry, and nonfiction. In the grade 3 book, each reading within a genre has been carefully selected or tailored for third-grade reading accessibility and interest. The stories and poems for the *Jacob's Ladder* curriculum at each grade level were chosen with three basic criteria in mind: (1) concrete to abstract development, (2) level of vocabulary, and (3) age-appropriate themes. The readings and exercises are designed to move students forward in their abstract thinking processes by promoting critical and creative thinking. The vocabulary in each reading is grade-level appropriate; however, when new or unfamiliar words are encountered, they should be covered in class before readings and ladder questions are assigned. Themes also are appropriate to the students' ages at each grade level and were chosen to complement themes typically seen in texts for each particular level. The short stories, poetry, and nonfiction readings with corresponding ladder sets are delineated in Part II. Table 2 outlines all grade 3 readings by genre.

Rationale

Constructing meaning of the written word is one of the earliest tasks required of students in schools. This skill occupies the central place in the curriculum at the elementary level. Yet, approaches to teaching reading comprehension often are "skill and drill," using worksheets about low-level reading material. As a result, students frequently are unable to transfer these skills from exercise pages and apply them to new higher level reading material.

The time expended to ensure that students become autonomous and advanced readers would suggest the need for a methodology that deliberately moves students from simple to complex reading skills with grade-

TABLE 2
Reading Selections by Genre

Short Stories	Poetry	Nonfiction
The Ant and the Dove	The Sound of Rain	Ancient Rome
The Crow and the Pitcher	Winter Shavings	The Circle of Life
Daedalus and Icarus	Owl	Geometry All Around Us
The Dog and His Reflection	Fog	The Industrial Revolution
The Fisherman and His Wife	Those Days Ago	What's the Chance?
How the Camel Got His Hump	Summer Song	A World of Resources
The Lion and the Gnat	Summer in the South	
The Mice in Council	Dandelions	
The North Wind and the Sun	Windy Nights	
Favorite Secret Place	Aloft	

appropriate texts. Such a learning approach to reading skill development ensures that students can traverse easily from basic comprehension skills to higher level critical reading skills, while using the same reading stimulus to navigate this transition. Reading comprehension is enhanced by instructional scaffolding, moving students from lower order to higher order thinking, using strategies and processes to help students analyze passages (Fisher & Frey, 2014; Peterson & Taylor, 2012). In addition, teachers who emphasize higher order thinking through questions and tasks such as those at the higher rungs of each ladder promote greater reading growth (Degener & Berne, 2016). *Jacob's Ladder* was written in response to teacher findings that students needed additional scaffolding to work consistently at higher levels of thinking in reading.

In addition, the adoption of the Common Core State Standards (CCSS) in 2010, or state standards that mimicked the CCSS, resulted in a new emphasis on the close reading of complex text. This involves making annotations, using text-dependent questions, and holding discussions about texts. Harvey and Goudvis (2007) have promoted the use of text coding and annotating as methods for students to deepen comprehension. In order to focus students' attention on specific elements of text in multiple readings, researchers have emphasized the need for teachers to provide text-dependent questions (Fisher & Frey, 2012; Lapp, Grant, Moss, & Johnson, 2013; Santori & Belfatti, 2017). Text-based discussion can facilitate reading comprehension by allowing students to construct their understanding of ideas in collaboration with their classmates (DeFrance & Fahrenbruck, 2015). Researchers have also noted the importance of discussions for enhancing student talk about texts and improving the comprehension of text (Duke, Pearson, Strachan, & Billman, 2011; Lawrence & Snow, 2011). Most of the questions in *Jacob's Ladder* are text-dependent questions. Discussions may be done in dyads, small groups, or with the entire class. Although *Jacob's Ladder* does not specifically address text coding or annotating, those are strategies that could easily be incorporated as students read the selections.

The *Jacob's Ladder* program is a compilation of the instructional scaffolding and reading exercises necessary to aid students in their journey toward becoming critical readers. Students learn concept development skills through learning to generalize, predicting and forecasting skills through delineating implications of events, and literary analysis skills through discerning textual meaning. The questions and tasks for each reading are open-ended, as this type of approach to responding to literature improves performance on comprehension tests (Wasik & Hindman, 2013). Progressing through the hierarchy of skills also requires students to reread the text, thereby improving metacomprehension accuracy (Hedin & Conderman, 2010).

Research Base

A quasi-experimental study was conducted using *Jacob's Ladder* as a supplementary program for students in Title I schools, grades 3–5. After professional development occurred, experimental teachers were instructed to implement the *Jacob's Ladder* curriculum in addition to their basal reading series and guided reading groups. Teachers in the control group taught their district-adopted textbook reading series as the main curriculum.

Findings from this study ($N = 495$) suggest that when compared to students who used the basal reader only, those students who were exposed to the *Jacob's Ladder* curriculum showed significant gains in reading comprehension and critical thinking. Likewise, students who used the curriculum showed significant and important growth on curriculum-based assessments that included determining implications/consequences, making inferences, outlining themes and generalizations, and applying creative synthesis. Students reported greater interest in reading and alluded that the curriculum made them "think harder." Teachers reported more in-depth student discussion and personal growth in the ability to ask open-ended questions when reading (Stambaugh, 2007).

Implementation Considerations

Teachers need to consider certain issues when implementing the *Jacob's Ladder* curriculum. Although the program is targeted for promising students who need more exposure to higher level thinking skills in reading, the program may be suitable for learners who are functioning above or below grade level.

As modeling, coaching, and feedback appear to enhance student growth in reading and writing (Fisher & Frey, 2015), it is recommended that teachers review how to complete the task ladders with the entire class at least once, outlining expectations and record-keeping tasks, as well as modeling the process prior to assigning small-group or independent work. Students should complete the ladder tasks on their own paper or on the template provided in Appendix B. As students gain more confidence in the curriculum, the teacher should allow more independent work coupled with small-group or paired discussion, and then whole-group sharing with teacher feedback.

Completing these activities in dyads or small groups will facilitate discussions that stress collaborative reasoning, thereby fostering greater engagement and higher level thinking (Duke et al., 2011; Lawrence & Snow, 2011). The stories and accompanying ladder questions and activities also may be organized into a reading center in the classroom or utilized with reading groups during guided reading.

Process of Jacob's Ladder

The process of inquiry and feedback, as led and modeled by the teacher, is critical to the success of the program and student mastery of process skills. Teachers need to encourage and solicit multiple student responses and encourage dialogue about various perspectives and interpretations of a given text, requiring students to justify their answers with textual support and concrete examples. Student use of the ladders depends on teacher stance and modeling as well as student readiness. After teacher modeling, students should understand how to use the ladders as prescribed by the teacher. Sample follow-up questions such as those listed below can be used by the teacher and posted in the classroom to help guide student discussion.

- That's interesting; does anyone have a different idea?
- What in the story makes you say that?

- What do you think the author means by . . . ?

- What do you think are the implications or consequences of . . . ?

- Did anyone view that differently? How?

- Does anyone have a different point of view? Justify your answer.

- In the story I noticed that . . . Do you think that might have significance to the overall meaning?

- I heard someone say that he thought the poem (story) was about . . . What do you think? Justify your answer from the events of the story.

- Do you notice any key words that might be significant? Why?

- Do you notice any words that give you a mental picture? Do those words have significance? What might they symbolize?

- I agree with . . . because . . .

- I had a different idea than . . . because . . .

Grouping Students

Jacob's Ladder may be used in a number of different grouping patterns. The program should be introduced initially as a whole-group activity directed by the teacher with appropriate open-ended questions, feedback, and monitoring. After students have examined each type of ladder with teacher guidance, they should be encouraged to use the program by writing ideas independently, sharing with a partner, and then discussing the findings with a group. The dyad approach provides maximum opportunities for student discussion of the readings and collaborative decisions about the answers to questions posed. One purpose of the program is to solicit meaningful discussion of the text. Like-ability groups are recommended (Kulik & Kulik, 1992) for discussion.

Pre- and Postassessments and Grading

The pre- and postassessments included in Appendix A were designed as a diagnostic-prescriptive approach to guide program implementation prior to the implementation of *Jacob's Ladder*. The pretest should be administered, scored, and then used to guide student instruction and the selection of readings for varied ability groups. Both the pre- and postassessment, scoring rubric, and sample exemplars for each rubric category and level are included in Appendix A along with exemplars to guide scoring.

In both the pre- and postassessments, students read a short passage and respond to the four questions. Question 1 focuses on implications and consequences (Ladder A); Question 2 on generalization, theme, and concept (Ladder B); Question 3 on inference (Ladder C); and Question 4 on creative synthesis (Ladder D). By analyzing each question and scored response, teachers may wish to guide reading selections toward the appropriate ladders and stories based on student need.

Upon conclusion of the program or as a midpoint check, the posttest may be administered to compare the pretest results and to measure growth in students' responses. These pre/post results could be used as part of a student portfolio, in a parent-teacher conference, or documentation of curriculum effectiveness and student progress. The pre- and postassessments were piloted to ensure that both forms were equivalent in difficulty (a = .76) and that the interrater reliability of scorers was appropriate (a = .81).

Student Reflection, Feedback, and Record Keeping

Students may use the Brainstorming/Answer Sheet provided in Appendix B for each ladder to record their personal thoughts independently before discussing with a partner. After finishing both of the ladders for each reading selection, a reflection page, My Reflection on Today's Reading and Discussion (also in Appendix B), can be provided, indicating the student's personal assessment of the work completed. Teachers also will want to check student answers as ladder segments are completed and conduct an error analysis. Individual or small-group consultation should occur at this time to ensure that students understand what they did incorrectly and why. In order to analyze student responses and progress across the program, teachers need to monitor student performance, using the student answer sheets to indicate appropriate completion of tasks. Specific comments about student work also are important to promote growth and understanding of content.

The Assessment/Response Form (Appendix B) may be used by the student as an answer sheet for a given ladder. The student may self-assess his or her work on the ladder in the form of a numerical score. The teacher may also provide a numerical score for feedback. In addition, there is space for both the student and the teacher to write comments about the student's work on the ladder.

Classroom Diagnostic Forms also are provided in Appendix B. On these forms, teachers record student progress on a 3-point scale: 2 (*exceeds expectations; applies skills very effectively*), 1 (*satisfactory; understands and applies skills*), or 0 (*needs improvement; needs more practice with the given skill set*) across readings and ladder sets. These forms can be used as part of a diagnostic-prescriptive approach to selecting reading materials and ladders based on student understanding or the need for more practice.

Sample Concluding Activities

Grading the ladders and responses are at the teacher's discretion. Many teachers use *Jacob's Ladder* for practice purposes only and do not grade them. As students initially learn how to complete *Jacob's Ladder* activities, teachers should provide feedback about their work, but not grades. If the teacher eventually decides to assign grades after students understand what to do, he or she should not overemphasize the lower rungs in graded activities. Lower rungs are intended only as a vehicle to the higher level questions at the top of the ladder. Instead, top rung questions may be used as a journal prompt or as part of a graded open-ended writing response. Grades also could be given based on guided discussion after students are trained on appropriate ways to discuss literature. Additional ideas for activities that could be graded are as follows:

- Write an opinion essay to justify what you think the story is about.
- Create a symbol to show the meaning of the story. Write a paragraph to justify your answer.
- In one word or phrase, tell what this story is mostly about. Justify your answer using examples from the story.
- Write a letter from the author's point of view, explaining the meaning of the story.
- Pretend you are an illustrator. Create a drawing for the story or poem that shows the main idea. Write a sentence that describes your illustration and the main idea.

Time Allotment

Although the time needed to complete *Jacob's Ladder* tasks will vary by student, most ladders should take students 15 minutes to read the selection and another 20–30 minutes to complete one ladder individually. More time is required for paired student and whole-group discussion of the questions. Teachers may wish to set aside 2 days each week for focusing on one *Jacob's Ladder* reading and the two commensurate ladders, especially when introducing the program.

Answer Key

An answer key is included at the end of the book. It contains a set of suggested answers for all questions related to each reading selection. All of the questions are somewhat open-ended; therefore, answers may vary. The answers provided in the key are simply suggestions to help illustrate the skills targeted by each ladder skill set.

Alignment to Standards

Tables 3, 4, and 5 contain alignment charts to demonstrate the connection of the fiction and nonfiction reading materials to relevant national standards in all subject areas. One of the benefits of this program is its ability to provide cross-disciplinary coverage of standards through the use of a single reading stimulus.

TABLE 3
Standards Alignment: Short Stories

Language Arts: Short Stories	The Ant and the Dove	The Crow and the Pitcher	Daedalus and Icarus	The Dog and His Reflection	The Fisherman and His Wife	How the Camel Got His Hump	The Lion and the Gnat	The Mice in Council	The North Wind and the Sun	Favorite Secret Place
The student will use analysis of text, including the interaction of the text with a reader's feelings and attitudes, to create a response.	✗	✗	✗	✗	✗	✗	✗	✗	✗	✗
The student will interpret and analyze the meaning of literary works from diverse cultures and authors by applying different critical lenses and analytic techniques.	✗	✗	✗	✗	✗	✗	✗	✗	✗	
The student will integrate various cues and strategies to comprehend what he or she reads.	✗	✗	✗	✗	✗	✗	✗	✗	✗	✗
The student will use a knowledge of the purposes, structures, and elements of writing to analyze and interpret various types of text.	✗	✗	✗	✗	✗	✗	✗	✗	✗	✗
Students will use word-analysis skills, context clues, and other strategies to read fiction and non-fiction with fluency and accuracy.	✗	✗	✗	✗	✗	✗	✗	✗	✗	✗

TABLE 4
Standards Alignment: Poetry

Language Arts: Poetry	The Sound of Rain	Winter Shavings	Owl	Fog	Those Days Ago	Summer Song	Summer in the South	Dandelions	Windy Nights	Aloft
The student will use analysis of text, including the interaction of the text with a reader's feelings and attitudes, to create a response.	✗	✗		✗		✗	✗			✗
The student will integrate various cues and strategies to comprehend what he or she reads.	✗	✗	✗	✗	✗	✗	✗	✗	✗	✗
The student will use a knowledge of the purposes, structures, and elements of writing to analyze and interpret various types of text.	✗	✗	✗	✗	✗	✗	✗	✗	✗	✗
Students will use word-analysis skills, context clues, and other strategies to read fiction and non-fiction with fluency and accuracy.	✗	✗	✗	✗	✗	✗	✗	✗	✗	✗

TABLE 5
Standards Alignment: Nonfiction

Social Studies, Science, and Math Standards: Nonfiction	Ancient Rome	The Circle of Life	Geometry All Around Us	The Industrial Revolution	What's the Chance?	A World of Resources
Social Studies Standards						
Culture				✘		
Time, Continuity, and Change	✘			✘		
People, Places, and Environments				✘		
Individual Development and Identity						
Individuals, Groups, and Institutions	✘					
Science, Technology, and Society				✘		
Science Standards						
Science as Inquiry						
Physical Science						
Life Science		✘				
Earth and Space Science						✘
Science and Technology						
Science in Personal and Social Perspectives						
History and Nature of Science						
Math Standards						
Number and Operations					✘	
Geometry			✘			
Measurement						
Data Analysis and Probability					✘	
Problem Solving					✘	
Communication						
Connections						

References

DeFrance, N. L., Fahrenbruck, M. L. (2015). Constructing a plan for text-based discussion. *Journal of Adolescent & Adult Literacy, 59,* 575–585. doi:10.1002/jaal.477

Degener, S., & Berne, J. (2016). Complex questions promote complex thinking. *The Reading Teacher, 70,* 595–599. doi:10.1002/trtr.1535

Duke, N. K., Pearson, P. D., Strachan, S. L., & Billman, A. K. (2011). Essential elements of fostering and teaching reading comprehension. In S. J. Samuels & A. E. Farstrup (Eds.), *What research has to say about reading instruction* (pp. 51–93). Newark, DE: International Reading Association. doi:10.1598/0829.03

Fisher, D., & Frey, N. (2012). Close reading in elementary schools. *The Reading Teacher, 66,*179–188. doi:10.1002/TRTR.01117

Fisher, D., & Frey, N. (2014). Scaffolded reading instruction of content-area texts. *The Reading Teacher, 67,* 347–351. doi:10.1002/trtr.1234

Fisher, D., & Frey, N. (2015). Teacher modeling using complex informational texts. *The Reading Teacher, 69*(1), 63–69. doi:10.1002/trtr.1372.

Harvey, S., & Goudvis, A. (2007). *Strategies that work: Teaching comprehension for understanding and engagement* (2nd ed.). Portland, ME: Stenhouse Publishers.

Hedin, L. R., & Conderman, G. (2010). Teaching students to comprehend informational text through rereading. *The Reading Teacher, 63,* 556–565. doi:10.1598/RT.63.7.3

Kulik, J. A., & Kulik, C.-L. C. (1992). Meta-analytic findings on grouping programs. *Gifted Child Quarterly, 36,* 73–77.

Lawrence, J. F., & Snow, C. E. (2011). Oral discourse and reading. In M. L. Kamil, P. D. Pearson, E. B. Moje, & P. P. Afflerbach (Eds.), *Handbook of reading research* (Vol. 4, pp. 320–337). New York, NY: Routledge.

Lapp, D., Grant, M., Moss, B., & Johnson, K. (2013). Close reading of science texts: What's now? What's next? *The Reading Teacher, 67,* 109–119.

Peterson, D. S., & Taylor, B. M. (2012). Using higher order questioning to accelerate students' growth in reading. *The Reading Teacher, 65,* 295–304. doi:10.1002/TRTR.01045

Santori, D., & Belfatti, M. (2017). Do text-dependent questions need to be teacher-dependent? Close reading from another angle. *The Reading Teacher, 70,* 649–657. doi:10.1002/trtr.1555

Stambaugh, T. (2007). *Effects of the Jacob's Ladder Reading Comprehension Program* (Unpublished doctoral dissertation). William & Mary. Williamsburg, VA.

Taba, H. (1962). *Curriculum development: Theory and practice.* NY: Harcourt, Brace & World.

Wasik, B. A., & Hindman, A. H. (2013). Realizing the promise of open-ended questions. *The Reading Teacher, 67,* 302–311. doi:10.1002/trtr.1218

Part II: Readings and Student Ladder Sets

Chapter 1: Short Stories and Corresponding Ladders
Chapter 2: Poetry and Corresponding Ladders
Chapter 3: Nonfiction and Corresponding Ladders

CHAPTER 1

Short Stories

Chapter 1 includes the selected readings and accompanying question sets for each short story selection. Each reading is followed by one or two sets of questions; each set is aligned to one of the four ladder skills.

For *Jacob's Ladder, Grade 3*, the skills covered by each selection are as follows:

Title	Ladder Skills
The Ant and the Dove	A, B
The Crow and the Pitcher	A, C
Daedalus and Icarus	A, C
The Dog and His Reflection	A, C
The Fisherman and His Wife	A
How the Camel Got His Hump	A
The Lion and the Gnat	A, C
The Mice in Council	A, C
The North Wind and the Sun	A, B
Favorite Secret Place	A, C

The Ant and the Dove

Originally told by Aesop

A thirsty ant crawled to the edge of the river to quench its thirst. The rapidly moving stream snatched the ant as it rushed by and almost drowned it. A white dove sitting on a tree plucked a leaf and let it fall into the stream close to him. The ant climbed on the leaf and floated to safety on the bank of the river. Not long after this event, a hunter came and stood under the same tree from which the dove had watched the struggling ant. The hunter sighted the dove and drew his bow to pierce his target. The ant, perceiving his plan, stung him on his foot. The hunter cried out in pain and dropped his bow. The noise made the dove fly away.

Moral: One good turn deserves another.

Consequences and Implications

A3

What were the overall consequences of the Dove's actions?

Cause and Effect

A2

There are several cause-and-effect relationships in the fable.
Complete the chart below, outlining causes and effects in the tale.

Cause	Effect

Sequencing

A1

List the events in the order they occur in the story.

THE ANT AND THE DOVE

Generalizations

B3

"One good turn deserves another" is a generalization about this fable.

Write another generalization about the fable
that you think is important.

Classifications

B2

What are the "good turns" that occur in the fable? Why
is each a "good turn"? Fill in the following table.

Good Turn	Why?

Details

B1

What are some images you picture when you read this fable?
Which phrases support those pictures? List at least four.

THE ANT AND THE DOVE

The Crow and the Pitcher

Originally told by Aesop

A crow, dying of thirst, came upon a pitcher that once had been full of water. When the crow put his beak into the mouth of the pitcher, he found that only very little water was left in it, and he could not reach far enough to get at it. He tried and tried, but at last had to give up in despair.

Then a thought came to him. He took a pebble and dropped it into the pitcher. Then he took another pebble and dropped it into the pitcher. Then he took another pebble and dropped it into the pitcher. Then he took another pebble and dropped it into the pitcher. Then he took another pebble and dropped it into the pitcher. At last he saw the water ris- ing toward him, and after casting a few more pebbles into the pitcher, he was able to drink and save his life.

Consequences and Implications

A3

What would have happened if the crow had done the following:
- Kept putting his beak in the pitcher?
- Flown away?
- Broken the pitcher?
- Waited for rain?

Cause and Effect

A2

What caused the water to reach the crow? What overall effect did it have on the crow?

Sequencing

A1

What steps did the crow use to get water? List them below in order:

1. _____
2. _____
3. _____
4. _____

THE CROW AND THE PITCHER

Main Idea, Theme, or Concept

C3

Main Idea: What is the main idea of this story?

Inference

C2

What made the crow successful in getting a drink of water? Why did his plan work?

Literary Elements

C1

What are the crow's most important qualities? What other characters have you read about that show similar life qualities? How were their situations similar to or different from the crow's situation?

THE CROW AND THE PITCHER

Daedalus and Icarus

Once upon a time in Ancient Greece, there was an architect by the name of Daedalus who loved his son and his work above all else. When the king of the island of Crete entrusted Daedalus with the job of designing and building his new palace, Daedalus was overjoyed and took his son, Icarus, to accompany him on the new project. He worked long and hard; the palace he built was nothing short of spectacular—the gardens were as beautiful as in a fairy tale, the living quarters were fit for a king, and there was an underground labyrinth that was supposed to be kept secret. The king inspected the finished project and loved it. Daedalus thought his job was through and started packing his and Icarus's belongings for the trip back home. The king, however, had other plans. If he was to ensure the labyrinth would be kept a secret, then he could not allow Daedalus and Icarus to leave! Trying to be nice, the king provided the architect and Icarus luxurious living space in the highest tower of the new palace, fine foods, even servants. None of it, however, could replace their freedom or their home.

Wise and patient, Daedalus started feeding wild birds on a windowsill. Every day as the birds ate, they shed a few feathers. After a while, Daedalus had collected a lot of feathers and some leftover wax candles. As part of an escape plan, Daedalus fashioned two sets of wings with the feathers set in wax. Donning one, he gave the other set to his son, Icarus, but warned him: "Don't fly too low or the sea will soak your feathers. Don't fly too high or the sun will melt your wax."

Together they flew from their prison, up into the air. Icarus beat his arms and soared after his father. The sea shimmered below him. To fly, he thought! To soar with the gulls! He loved it. Icarus grew so excited by his new power, he flew upward toward the clouds, forgetting his father's warning.

Suddenly, a feather loosened from his artificial wings. Then another fell off. He stared at them. The wax was melting fast! His wings were coming apart! He had flown too close to the sun!

At this very moment Daedalus turned and could do nothing but watch helplessly as the wax melted from Icarus's wings, and Icarus plummeted to the unforgiving sea.

Consequences and Implications

A3

What implications might this myth have for your own life? For society?

Cause and Effect

A2

What was the effect of Icarus not heeding his father's warning and flying too close to the sun?

Sequencing

A1

List the events that occurred in this myth as you read them in the text (in order).

Main Idea, Theme, or Concept

Theme: How is freedom a theme in this myth?
Express your understanding by filling in as many bubbles
as you can in the following diagram.

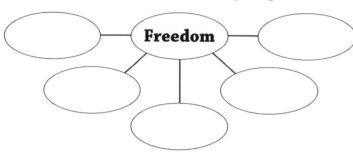

Inference

Why do you think Icarus did not obey his father's instructions?

Literary Elements

List all of the characters in the myth and their relationships
to each other. Use the chart below to help you.

Character	Relationship

What is the setting (place and time) of "Daedalus and Icarus"?

C3

C2

C1

DAEDALUS AND ICARUS

The Dog and His Reflection
Originally told by Aesop

A dog, to whom the butcher had thrown a bone, was hurrying home with his prize as fast as he could go. As he crossed a narrow footbridge, he happened to look down and saw himself reflected in the quiet water as if in a mirror. But the greedy dog thought he saw a real dog carrying a bone much bigger than his own.

If he had stopped to think, he would have known better. But instead of thinking, he dropped his bone and sprang at the dog in the river, only to find himself swimming for dear life to reach the shore. At last he managed to scramble out, and as he stood sadly thinking about the good bone he had lost, he realized what a stupid dog he had been.

Moral: It is very foolish to be greedy.

A3

Consequences and Implications

- What "price" did the dog pay for his actions in the story?
- What did he lose? (Think of all of the possibilities!)
- What do you think he will do the next time he sees his reflection?

A2

Cause and Effect

- What *caused* the dog to lose his bone?
- What *effect* did it have on him?
- Draw a before and after cartoon picture of the dog and write a caption for each cartoon.

A1

Sequencing

Make a list of events in the story, beginning with what happens first, then second, and so forth.

THE DOG AND HIS REFLECTION

Main Idea, Theme, or Concept

C3

Main Idea: What important ideas does the story tell us?

Inference

C2

What inference do you make from the sentence: "But the greedy dog thought he saw a real dog carrying a bone much bigger than his own"?

Literary Elements

C1

What qualities does the dog possess? Make a chart illustrating both the positive and negative aspects of each quality you identify.

Qualities	Positive	Negative

THE DOG AND HIS REFLECTION

The Fisherman and His Wife

By Jacob Grimm and Wilhelm Grimm

There once was a fisherman and his wife who lived together in a hut by the seashore. The fisherman went out every day with his hook and line to catch fish, and he angled and angled.

One day he was sitting with his rod, looking into the clear water, when suddenly down went the line to the bottom of the water. When he drew it up, he found a great fish on the hook.

The fish said to him, "Fisherman, listen to me. Let me go. I am not a real fish but an enchanted prince. What good shall I be to you if you land me? I shall not taste good. So put me back into the water again and let me swim away."

"Well," said the fisherman, "no need of so many words about the matter. As you can speak, I had much rather let you swim away." So he cast him back into the sea. Then the fisherman went home to his wife in the hut.

"Well, husband," said the wife, "have you caught anything today?"

"No," said the man. "That is, I did catch a huge fish, but as he said he was an enchanted prince, I let him go again."

"Did you not wish for something?" asked his wife.

"No," said the man. "What should I wish for?"

"Oh dear!" said the wife. "It is so dreadful always to live in this hut. You might as well have wished for a little cottage. I daresay he'd give it to us. Go and be quick."

When he went back, the sea was green and yellow and not nearly so clear. So he stood and said:

> Oh, man of the sea, come listen to me,
> For Alice, my wife, the plague of my life,
> Has sent me to ask a boon of thee.

Then the fish came swimming up and said, "Now then, what does she want?"

"Oh," said the man, "my wife says that I should have asked you for something when I caught you. She does not want to live any longer in the hut and would rather have a cottage."

"Go home," said the fish. "She has it already."

So the man went home and found, instead of the hut, a little cottage, and his wife was

sitting on a bench before the door. She took him by the hand and said to him, "Come in and see if this is not a great deal better." They went in, and there was a little sitting room and a beautiful little bedroom, a kitchen and a larder, with all sorts of furniture, and iron and brassware of the very best. And, at the back was a little yard with chickens and ducks, and a little garden full of green vegetables and fruit.

"Look," said the wife, "is not that nice?"

"Yes," said the man. "If this can only last, we shall be happy the rest of our days."

"We will see about that," said his wife.

All went well for a week or fortnight. Then the wife said, "Look here, husband, the cottage is really too small. I think the fish had better give us a larger house. I should like very much to live in a large stone castle. So go to your fish, and he will send us a castle."

"Oh, my dear wife!" said the man. "The cottage is good enough. What do we want a castle for?"

"Go along," said the wife. "He might just as well give it to us as not. Do as I say."

The man did not want to go, and he said to himself, "It is not the right thing to do."

Nevertheless he went. When he came to the seaside, the water was purple and dark blue and gray and dark, and not green and yellow as before. And he stood and said:

> Oh, man of the sea, come listen to me,
> For Alice, my wife, the plague of my life,
> Has sent me to ask a boon of thee.

"Now then, what does she want?" asked the fish.

"Oh!" said the man, half-frightened. "She wants to live in a large stone castle."

"Go home. She is already standing before the door," said the fish.

Then the man went home, as he supposed. But when he arrived, there stood in the place of the cottage a great castle of stone, and his wife was standing on the steps about to go in. So she took him by the hand and said, "Let us enter."

With that he went in with her. In the castle was a great hall with a marble floor, and there were a great many servants, who led them through the large door. The passages were decked with tapestry and the rooms with golden chairs and tables. Crystal chandeliers were hanging from the ceiling, and all the rooms had carpets. The tables were spread with the most delicious foods for anyone who wanted them. At the back of the house was a stable yard for horses and cattle and carriages of the finest. Besides, there was a splendid large garden with the most beautiful flowers and fine fruit trees, and also a park, for half a mile long, with deer, oxen, sheep, and everything the heart could wish for.

"There," said the wife, "is not this beautiful?"

"Oh, yes," said the man. "If it will only last, we can live in this fine castle and be very well contented."

"We will see about that," said the wife.

The next morning the wife awakened at the break of day, and she looked out of her window and saw the beautiful country lying all around.

"Husband," she called, "look out of the window. Just think if we could be King over all this country. Go to your fish and tell him we should like to be King."

"Now, wife," said the man. "What should we be Kings for? I don't want to be King."

"Well," said the wife, "if you don't want to be King, I will be. You must go at once to the fish. I must be King."

So the man went, very much put out that his wife should want to be King. He did not at all want to go, and yet he went all the same.

When he came to the sea, the water was dark and gray and rushed far inland, and he stood there and said:

> Oh, man of the sea, come listen to me,
> For Alice, my wife, the plague of my life,
> Has sent me to ask a boon of thee.

"Now then, what does she want?" asked the fish.

"Oh, dear!" said the man. "She wants to be King."

"Go home. She is so already," said the fish.

So the man went back, and as he came to the palace, he saw it was very much larger and had great towers and splendid gateways. The herald stood before the door, and there were a number of soldiers with kettledrums and trumpets.

When he came inside, everything was of marble and gold, and there were many curtains with great gold tassels. Then he went through the doors to the throne room, and there was his wife, sitting upon a throne of gold and diamonds, and she had a great golden crown on her head, and the scepter in her hand was of pure gold and jewels, and on each side stood six pages in a

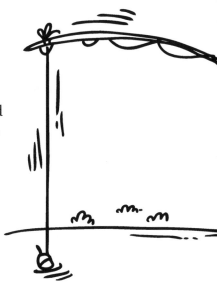

row, each one a head shorter than the other. So the man went up to her and said, "Well, wife, so now you are King."

"Yes," said she. "Now I am King."

Then he stood and looked at her, and when he had gazed at her for some time he said, "Well, wife, this is fine for you to be King. Now there is nothing more to ask for."

"Oh, husband!" said the wife, seeming quite restless. "I am tired of this already. Go to your fish and tell him that now I am King, I must be Emperor."

"Now, wife," said the man, "what do you want to be Emperor for?"

"Husband," said she, "go and tell the fish I want to be Emperor."

"Oh, dear!" said the man. "He could not do it. I cannot ask him such a thing. There is but one Emperor at a time. The fish can't possibly make anyone Emperor—indeed he can't."

"Now, look here," said the wife, "I am King, and you are only my husband, so will you go at once? Go along. For if he was able to make me King he is able to make me Emperor, and I will and must be Emperor. So go along."

So he was obliged to go. And as he went he felt very uncomfortable about it, and he thought to himself, "It is not at all the right thing to do. To want to be Emperor is going too far; the fish will soon get tired of this."

With this he came to the sea, and the water was quite black, and the foam flew, and the wind blew, and the man was terrified. But he stood and said:

> Oh, man of the sea, come listen to me,
> For Alice, my wife, the plague of my life,
> Has sent me to ask a boon of thee.

"What is it now?" asked the fish.

"Oh, dear!" said the man. "My wife wants to be Emperor."

"Go home," said the fish. "She is Emperor already."

So the man went home and found the castle adorned with polished marble and golden gates. The troops were being marshaled before the door, and they were blowing trumpets and beating drums. And when he entered he saw barons, earls, and dukes waiting about like servants, and the doors were of bright gold. He saw his wife sitting upon a throne of solid gold, and it was about 2 miles high. She had a great golden crown on, set in precious stones, and in one hand she had a scepter, and in the other a globe; and on both sides of her stood pages in two rows, all arranged according to size, from the enormous giant of 2 miles high, to the tiniest dwarf the size of my little finger, and before her stood earls and dukes in crowds.

So the man went up to her and said, "Well, wife, so now you are Emperor. I hope you are contented at last."

"We will see about that," said his wife.

With that they went to bed. But she was as far as ever from being contented, and she could not get to sleep for thinking of what she would like to be next.

The next morning as she sat before the window watching the sun rise, she said, "Oh, I have it! What if I should make the sun and moon to rise? Husband," she called, "wake up and go to your fish and tell him I want power over the sun and moon."

"Oh, wife!" said the man. "The fish cannot do that. Do be contented, I beg of you."

But she became most impatient and said, "I can wait no longer. Go at once."

So off he went, as well as he could for fright. And a dreadful storm arose, so that he could hardly keep on his feet. The houses and trees were blown down, and the mountains trembled, and rocks fell in the sea. The sky was quite black; and it thundered and lightning flashed; and the waves, crowned with foam, ran mountains high. So he cried out:

> Oh, man of the sea, come listen to me,
> For Alice, my wife, the plague of my life,
> Has sent me to ask a boon of thee.

"Well, what now?" said the fish.

"Oh, dear!" said the man. "She wants to order about the sun and the moon."

"Go home with you," said the fish, "And you will find her in the old hut."

And there they are sitting to this very day.

Consequences and Implications

A3

What were the consequences for the wife of her continued demands on the enchanted fish?

Cause and Effect

A2

What effect did the husband's continued willingness to take his wife's demands to the fish have on his wife's actions?

Sequencing

A1

The following events from the story are not in order.
How would you sequence them to tell the story?

- The wife wanted to be emperor.
- The fisherman caught an enchanted fish.
- The wife wanted a cottage.
- The wife told the fisherman he should have asked the fish to grant him a wish.
- The sea was black and the wind was blowing.
- The wife was returned to the hut in which she and the fisherman originally lived.
- The sea was green and yellow.

How The Camel Got His Hump
by Rudyard Kipling

Now this is the next tale, and it tells how the Camel got his big hump.

In the beginning of years, when the world was so new and all, and the Animals were just beginning to work for Man, there was a Camel, and he lived in the middle of a Howling Desert because he did not want to work; and besides, he was a Howler himself. So he ate sticks and thorns and tamarisks and milkweed and prickles, most 'scruciating idle; and when anybody spoke to him he said "Humph!" Just "Humph!" and no more.

Presently the Horse came to him on Monday morning, with a saddle on his back and a bit in his mouth, and said, "Camel, O Camel, come out and trot like the rest of us."

"Humph!" said the Camel; and the Horse went away and told the Man.

Presently the Dog came to him, with a stick in his mouth, and said, "Camel, O Camel, come and fetch and carry like the rest of us."

"Humph!" said the Camel; and the Dog went away and told the Man.

Presently the Ox came to him, with the yoke on his neck and said, "Camel, O Camel, come and plough like the rest of us."

"Humph!" said the Camel; and the Ox went away and told the Man.

At the end of the day the Man called the Horse and the Dog and the Ox together, and said, "Three, O Three, I'm very sorry for you (with the world so new-and-all); but that Humph-thing in the Desert can't work, or he would have been here by now, so I am going to leave him alone, and you must work double-time to make up for it."

That made the Three very angry (with the world so new-and-all), and they held a palaver, and an *indaba*, and a *punchayet*, and a pow-wow on the edge of the Desert; and the Camel came chewing milkweed *most* 'scruciating idle, and laughed at them. Then he said "Humph!" and went away again.

Presently there came along the Djinn in charge of All Deserts, rolling in a cloud of dust (Djinns always travel that way because it is Magic), and he stopped to palaver and pow-wow with the Three.

"Djinn of All Deserts," said the Horse, "is it right for any one to be idle, with the world so new-and-all?"

"Certainly not," said the Djinn. "Well," said the Horse, "there's a thing in the middle of your Howling Desert (and he's a Howler himself) with a long neck and long legs, and he hasn't done a stroke of work since Monday morning. He won't trot."

"Whew!" said the Djinn, whistling, "that's my Camel, for all the gold in Arabia! What does he say about it?"

"He says 'Humph!'" said the Dog; "and he won't fetch and carry."

"Does he say anything else?"

"Only 'Humph!'; and he won't plough," said the Ox.

"Very good," said the Djinn. "I'll humph him if you will kindly wait a minute."

The Djinn rolled himself up in his dust-cloak, and took a bearing across the desert, and found the Camel most 'scruciatingly idle, looking at his own reflection in a pool of water.

"My long and bubbling friend," said the Djinn, "what's this I hear of your doing no work, with the world so new-and-all?"

"Humph!" said the Camel.

The Djinn sat down, with his chin in his hand, and began to think a Great Magic, while the Camel looked at his own reflection in the pool of water.

"You've given the Three extra work ever since Monday morning, all on account of your 'scruciating idleness," said the Djinn; and he went on thinking Magics, with his chin in his hand.

"Humph!" said the Camel.

"I shouldn't say that again if I were you," said the Djinn; "you might say it once too often. Bubbles, I want you to work."

And the Camel said "Humph!" again; but no sooner had he said it than he saw his back, that he was so proud of, puffing up and puffing up into a great big lolloping humph.

"Do you see that?" said the Djinn. "That's your very own humph that you've brought upon your very own self by not working. To-day is Thursday, and you've done no work since Monday, when the work began. Now you are going to work."

"How can I," said the Camel, "with this humph on my back?"

"That's made a-purpose," said the Djinn, "all because you missed those three days. You will be able to work now for three days without eating, because you can live on your humph; and don't you ever say I never did anything for you. Come out of the Desert and go to the Three, and behave. Humph yourself!"

And the Camel humphed himself, humph and all, and went away to join the Three. And from that day to this the Camel always wears a humph (we call it "hump" now, not to hurt his feelings); but he has never yet caught up with the three days that he missed at the beginning of the world, and he has never yet learned how to behave.

Consequences and Implications

A3

What were the consequences of the humph growing on the Camel's back?

Cause and Effect

A2

What effect did the Camel's refusal to work have on the Horse, Dog, and Ox?

Sequencing

A1

The following events from the story are not in order.
How would you sequence them to tell the story?

- The Camel sat idly in the desert and looked at his reflection in a pool of water.
- The Camel ate sticks and thorns and answered anyone who spoke to him with "Humph!"
- The Camel said "Humph" too many times, and a hump grew on his back.
- Man called the Horse and the Dog and the Ox together to talk about their work.
- The Djinn stopped to talk with the Horse and the Dog and the Ox.
- The Dog asked the Camel to help with the work.
- The Djinn tried to get the Camel to work.

HOW THE CAMEL GOT HIS HUMP

The Lion and the Gnat

Originally told by Aesop

A lion was enraged by a gnat that was buzzing around his head, but the gnat was not the least disturbed. "Do you think," he said spitefully, "that I am afraid of you because they call you king?" Then he flew at the lion and stung him sharply on the nose. In fury the lion struck at the gnat, but only succeeded in tearing himself with his claws. Again and again the gnat stung the lion, who was now roaring terribly. At last, worn out with rage and covered with wounds made by his own teeth and claws, the lion gave up the fight. The gnat buzzed away to tell the whole world about his victory, but instead flew straight into a spider's web. There, he who had defeated the king of beasts came to a miserable end, the prey of a little spider.

Name: _____ Date: _____

Consequences and Implications

A3

What do you see as consequences of the following situations in life:
- Being smaller than other creatures?
- Being larger than other creatures?
- Being too clever?
- Being too proud?

Cause and Effect

A2

What caused the gnat to get caught? What effect did it have on him?

Sequencing

A1

Draw three scenes in sequence that depict the main events that happened in this story. Title each scene.

THE LION AND THE GNAT

C3 — Main Idea, Theme, or Concept

Theme: What major ideas does the story tell us? Write a story with human characters that is similar to this animal story.

C2 — Inference

What evidence is there in the story that the gnat was proud? Why did he feel this way?

C1 — Literary Elements

The main characters are a lion and a gnat. Complete a comparison chart to show how different they are.

Characters	Similarities	Differences
Lion		
Gnat		

The Mice in Council

Originally told by Aesop

Once upon a time, the mice, feeling constantly in danger from a cat, called a meeting to decide upon the best means of getting rid of this continual annoyance. Many plans were discussed and rejected. At last, a young mouse got up and proposed that a bell should be hung around the cat's neck, so that from then on they would always have advanced warning of her coming, and so be able to escape. This suggestion was hailed with the greatest applause and unanimous agreement. Upon which an old mouse, who had sat silent all the while, got up and said that he considered the plan most clever, and that it would, no doubt, solve their problem. But he had one question to ask: Which one of them was going to put the bell around the cat's neck?

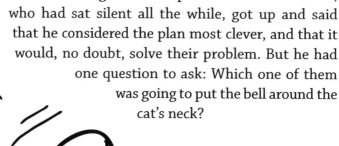

Name: _____ Date: _____

Consequences and Implications

A3

What implication might you make about "age and experience" based on the story?

Cause and Effect

A2

Complete the following chart:

In the story, the cat *caused*:	The *effect* was that the mice:

Sequencing

A1

Describe, in order, four steps the mice might take to put the bell on the cat.

THE MICE IN COUNCIL

Main Idea, Theme, or Concept

C3

Main Idea: What main idea does the story teach us
about groups? About how to solve problems?

Inference

C2

What inference do you draw from the last sentence: "Which one of them
was going to put the bell around the cat's neck?" What does it mean?

Literary Elements

C1

Why are cats and mice natural enemies? List qualities
and habits of each in the following chart.

	Qualities	Habits
Cats		
Mice		

THE MICE IN COUNCIL

The North Wind and the Sun
Originally told by Aesop

Over a period of time, the wind and the sun quarreled with one another. The wind, having great power and strong force, was convinced that he was stronger than the sun. He looked for every opportunity to prove his position. The sun, confident in her intense heat and awesome light, was sure that her powers were much greater than the powers or force of the wind.

It just so happened, on a particular day, a lone traveler was walking down a long, dusty road. The sun approached the wind and said: "I have a plan that will settle our quarrel as to which of us is the stronger." The wind stared at the sun in disbelief. What plan had the sun now concocted to prove she was the stronger?

The sun revealed her plan to the wind. "I believe that whichever one of us can cause that lone traveler to take off his coat shall be declared to be the stronger. In fact, I want to be very fair in this task, so I will let you go first."

The sun made her way behind a large black cloud, at which point the wind began to blow as hard as he could blow. He blew directly on the traveler, until the traveler wrapped his coat more closely around his body. No matter how hard the wind blew, it was in vain. The man only clung more tightly to his coat. Finally, in despair, the wind had to give up.

Coming out from behind the huge black cloud, the sun shone brightly with all of her intensity upon the weary traveler. The traveler, beginning to perspire from the heat of the direct sun, found it too hot to continue without relief. At this point he stopped and took off his coat and continued on with his journey.

Moral: It is easier to use persuasion than try to win with force.

A3

Consequences and Implications

Think about the two ways the sun and the wind tried to influence the traveler. Why do you think the sun's method was more effective? Could the wind have done anything differently?

A2

Cause and Effect

What was the effect of the wind blowing forcefully on the traveler?

A1

Sequencing

What happened when the young wind blew the first time? The second time?

THE NORTH WIND AND THE SUN

THE NORTH WIND AND THE SUN

Generalizations

B3

What generalizations can you make about the relationship of power and persuasion?

Classifications

B2

Create two columns. In column one, list times when you have seen or read about persuasion being more powerful than force. In column two, list times you have seen or read about power winning over persuasion.

Details

B1

What was the strength of the wind?
What was the strength of the sun?
Which was stronger and why?

Favorite Secret Place
by Kendall Sieg

I can hear the water gurgling in the distance. The flat rock under me warms my body, along with the sun, climbing higher into the deep, light blue sky. It makes me feel warm and at peace, inside as well as out. When I look up, I see only a few clouds in the sky. They float toward the east, the gentle breeze blowing softly. It relaxes me, and it's hard to tell if they are moving at all. But if I look at them, then close my eyes for a very long time, I open them again, and the clouds are in a different location. I glance around, taking in my surroundings.

Next to me is a river, lapping gently at my rock, which I am sitting upon like a queen of the water. Across the river, there is a wide strip of sand, like a very, very small beach. There are small rocks and big rocks scattered and implanted in the sand. I imagine if there were people there, playing with the sand and rocks. It would spoil the secret, the privacy of nature. Rather than finding something to keep myself busy with, like playing in the sand, I simply enjoy the fact that it is there, and I am here, with it. A part of it. As I continue looking on, the sand gets drier the farther I look. Soon, the sand is dirt, reaching the edge of a forest. I examine the trees, searching for birds and squirrels. I see a few, but not many. I hear the birds, chirping and squalling, but I do not see them, as they are expertly hidden in the trees. They want to be hidden, secret. I respect that, the secret. The privacy. I understand and feel nature's presence.

I let my hand dangle over the water, the icy coldness rushing past my fingertips as they become numb. My eyes bore into the water, studying it, understanding it, and I see slick, dark figures pass by. They are so far, yet only a little ways from my hands. I see one smaller than the others, and my eyes follow it until it is not visible anymore. I let my gaze wander to the small waterfall emptying into a pool.

I feel sweat trickling down the side of my face. I lean over, and plunge my head into the water, letting the refreshing liquid freeze my face until I have to bring it back up again, gasping for air. But soon, the water evaporates, and I am sweating again, dipping my hands in the water, and rubbing my face to cool down. I look up at the sun, and see a bald eagle fly across the sky. Soon, another eagle has joined him, squalling and calling. They hook their feet together and spin in a circle, falling closer and closer to the surface of the Earth. But before they hit the ground, they separate and fly toward the sky. It makes me feel special, yet not worthy, that I witnessed the beautifully magnificent moment. I look away, too heated by the scorching sun to sit on the rock any longer.

I walk over to the edge of the pool. Staring into the water, I walk to the top of the mini waterfall. I take a few steps back, feeling the cool water glide between my feet, cooling my body. I feel at peace, calm, in this beautiful scene of wilderness. I begin to run, and I leap off the top of the waterfall. As I am in the air, I glance below me. I see rough water knocking off jagged rocks. I also see smooth water sliding off the rocks so delicately. I see trees around me, and a river flowing straight down the mountain in front of me. Faded mountains sit on the horizon, the sun just above them. I don't have time to absorb anything else, because just then, I crash onto the surface of the water.

Note. Originally published in *Creative Kids* magazine, Summer 2015. Reprinted with permission of Prufrock Press.

Consequences and Implications

A3

What would have happened if the narrator did not appreciate nature? How would it have changed the story?

Cause and Effect

A2

What *effect* did plunging her face into the water have on the narrator? Think of a time when you have done something like that. How was your reaction similar to or different from that of the narrator?

Sequencing

A1

List four important events from the story in order.

FAVORITE SECRET PLACE

Main Idea, Theme, or Concept

C3

Main Idea: What is the main idea of "Favorite Secret Place"?

Inference

C2

What evidence or details in the story tell you
that the narrator loved nature?

Literary Elements

C1

What are some examples of how the narrator uses words
to create mental images (imagery) for the reader?

FAVORITE SECRET PLACE

CHAPTER 2

Poetry

Chapter 2 includes the selected readings and accompanying question sets for each poetry selection. Each reading is followed by one set of questions aligned to one of the four ladder skills.

For *Jacob's Ladder, Grade 3*, the skills covered by each selection are as follows:

Title	Ladder Skills
The Sound of Rain	C
Winter Shavings	C
Owl	C
Fog	B
Those Days Ago	B
Summer Song	C
Summer in the South	A
Dandelions	B
Windy Nights	A
Aloft	C

The Sound of Rain

by Emily Yao

Rain.
Slowly dripping
down, pitter-patter,
pitter-patter,
a musical rhythm
inside my
head.
When I look
up,
glimmers of
light seep through
mad, ferocious
clouds
of black and grey.
When I look
down,
puddles of water
collect
on the mushy, wet grass,
reflecting my
image like a
mirror
on a wall.
A drop falls,
then another,
another,
again and again.
My reflection ripples in a
pool of rain.
Wind whistles and winds
around me,
slapping me on my
cheek.
Rain.
Slowly dripping
down, pitter-patter,
pitter-patter,
a musical rhythm
inside my
head.

Note. Originally published in *Creative Kids* magazine, Spring 2016. Reprinted with permission of Prufrock Press.

Main Idea, Theme, or Concept

C3

Main Idea: What is the main idea of this poem?

Inference

C2

The author seems to be outside during a
storm. What words tell you this?

Literary Elements

C1

What is the author's tone when she writes
about rain? What words tell you this?

THE SOUND OF RAIN

Winter Shavings

by Ellen Zhang

A small and naïve child,
With pure white wondering eyes,
Falling, spiraling
Into a blanket,
Of soft silence, rippling
The small snowflake starts
To float slowly
Gravity stops it, but it
Is a snowflake and
It's already frozen

Note. Originally published in *Creative Kids* magazine, Winter 2014. Reprinted with permission of Prufrock Press.

C3

Main Idea, Theme, or Concept

Main Idea: How does the title give the reader a clue about the main idea of the poem? Explain your answer using words from the poem.

C2

Inference

"Winter Shavings"
What does the author mean by this title? What can be inferred about the snowflakes from this title?

C1

Literary Elements

- Make a list of phrases or words that describe snow.
- How does the author use those words and phrases to put a picture in your head? What do you "see"? Why?
- Illustrate your vision of the poem based on the descriptive language used.

Owl

by Iris Kreilkamp

The last of the animals
Slip silently into crevices.
The last door closes,
The last light flickers off,
And an ancient song
Fills the air,
Dripping like velvety paint
Over a dark landscape.
The stars open their eyes,
Awakened by this blanket
Of soft, heavy sound.
The owl sings.

Note. Originally published in *Creative Kids* magazine, Summer 2015. Reprinted with permission of Prufrock Press.

Main Idea, Theme, or Concept

C3

Theme: Write a poem like "Owl" to describe an animal you like. (Use the poem as your model.)

Inference

C2

What evidence is important for indicating that the animal being described is an owl?

Literary Elements

C1

What words does the poet use to describe the owl's song?

OWL

Fog

By Carl Sandburg

The fog comes
On little cat feet.

It sits looking
Over harbor and city
On silent haunches
And then moves on.

Generalizations

B3

Can you create a poem that is like this one? Choose one natural element and one animal from the following table to help you.

Natural Elements	Animal
Sun	Dog
Fire	Horse
Wind	Bird
Rain	Fish

Classifications

B2

The author chooses a cat to describe the fog. What characteristics of cats might have made the author choose it? Make a list of these cat characteristics.

FOG

Details

B1

Draw a picture that might go along with the poem. Write a sentence to explain your picture.

Those Days Ago
by Anne Cao

Do you remember the time when I was young?
Do you remember the time at the beach?
The splash and crash of the waves on the sand,
Tall sandcastles stood like valiant knights.
The seaweed was a mermaid's hair
Dancing swiftly through the waves.
The ocean shone like glass
Reflecting the heart of the sun.
And now I can reign
Upon the heat of the sand
Along with the crashing waves.
The beach was my kingdom
And I was its queen.

Note. Originally published in *Creative Kids* magazine, Summer 2015. Reprinted with permission of Prufrock Press.

Generalizations

B3

Generalizations are broad ideas that can apply to many situations. Write at least four generalizations you can make about the beach based on the poem and your list and your categories from Questions B2 and B1. You may use the chart below to help organize your ideas.

Generalization	Evidence From the Poem	Evidence From My List

Classifications

B2

Using your list from Question 2 in Section B1, develop categories for items found at the beach. Put each item into a category. How are your categories similar? How are they different?

Details

B1

"Those Days Ago" is about the beach. Draw a picture of at least one item described in the poem.

Brainstorm a list of items found at the beach. Write down at least 25.

Summer Song

by William Carlos Williams

Wanderer moon
smiling a
faintly ironical smile
at this
brilliant, dew-moistened
summer morning,—
a detached
sleepily indifferent
smile, a
wanderer's smile,—
if I should
buy a shirt
your color and
put on a necktie
sky-blue
where would they carry me?

Main Idea, Theme, or Concept

C3

Main Idea: What is the main idea of this poem?

Inference

C2

How does the poet imply that the summer moon is different or special? What lines from the poem support your inference?

Literary Elements

C1

Personification is a literary term used when writers give human characteristics to objects. Does the moon demonstrate human qualities in this poem? If so, how? Use text from the poem to support your answer.

SUMMER SONG

Summer in the South

by Paul Laurence Dunbar

The oriole sings in the greening grove
As if he were half-way waiting,
The rosebuds peep from their hoods of green,
Timid and hesitating.
The rain comes down in a torrent sweep
And the nights smell warm and piney,
The garden thrives, but the tender shoots
Are yellow-green and tiny.
Then a flash of sun on a waiting hill,
Streams laugh that erst were quiet,
The sky smiles down with a dazzling blue
And the woods run mad with riot.

Consequences and Implications

A3

What if the seasons never changed? What would be the consequences if it were always summer? What would be the consequences for people if it were always winter?

What does the poem imply about summer in the South? Support your answer.

Cause and Effect

A2

In "Summer in the South," the poet uses personification to give the different items in nature human-like qualities. The poet writes about things that change because summer arrives, such as "the nights smell warm and piney . . ." How does summer change things in nature? How do you know? Use lines from the poem to support your answer.

In one part of the poem, the author wrote: "Streams laugh that erst were quiet." In your opinion, what effect does the change in the streams have?

Sequencing

A1

The events that occur in nature during the summer are an important part of this poem. How does summer begin? How does it progress? Create and illustrate a timeline for the poem, making sure to sequence the events in the correct order.

Dandelions
by Neha Lenin

I am not one of them.

They will not accept me for who I am,
excluded from parties and conversations,
ignored and overlooked;

They leave me to wonder,
am I kind?
am I caring?
am I a good friend?
because I was told
"it's not what's on the outside but the inside that matters."

Or is it just because of my appearance
and inferior background,
that I am treated the way I am?

I am a dandelion in a field of daisies.
I am not popular, I am not one of them.

Note. Originally published in *Creative Kids* magazine, Spring 2017.
Reprinted with permission of Prufrock Press.

Generalizations

B3

Which word or phrase best explains the poem: (a) friendship or (b) being an individual? Why? Use words from the poem to explain your answer.

Classifications

B2

This poem has some words and phrases that are positive in meaning, and others that are more negative. Classify words or phrases found in the poem into the two groups: positive and negative.

Details

B1

Two students were arguing about what the poem meant. One student said it was about dandelions. Another student said the poem was about someone who didn't fit in too well with other children her age. Which student do you believe is correct? Make a list of words or phrases in the poem that help you know.

DANDELIONS

Windy Nights

By Robert Louis Stevenson

Whenever the moon and stars are set,
Whenever the wind is high,
All night long in the dark and wet,
A man goes riding by.
Late in the night when the fires are out,
Why does he gallop and gallop about?

Whenever the trees are crying aloud,
And ships are tossed at sea,
By, on the highway, low and loud,
By at the gallop he goes, and then
By he comes back at the gallop again.

Consequences and Implications

A3

Who is "he" in the poem? What clues do you
have that might imply who "he" is?

Cause and Effect

A2

Wind causes many things to happen. What happens in the poem as a
result of wind? Can you think of other effects that the wind causes?

Sequencing

A1

Which words does the author use multiple times? Do you think
those are important to the order of the poem? Why or why not?

WINDY NIGHTS

Aloft

by Miranda Sun

Our seabird is the truest ship
He floats on the skies
With feathery sails
And a light keel bone
His tail as a rudder
Friends with the wind
He perches in port
As swift as a current
He carries the ocean's song.

Note. Originally published in *Creative Kids* magazine, Summer 2015. Reprinted with permission of Prufrock Press.

Main Idea, Theme, or Concept

C3

Main Idea: What is the main idea of this poem?

Inference

C2

What evidence from the poem suggests that the author sees the seabird as a graceful animal?

Literary Elements

C1

The author uses a metaphor to compare the seabird to something else. Identify the metaphor. Describe what she is comparing the bird to in the poem. What other comparisons does she make to strengthen this comparison?

Identify the two similes in the poem.

ALOFT

CHAPTER
3

Nonfiction

Chapter 3 includes the selected readings and accompanying question sets for each nonfiction selection. Each reading is followed by one or two sets of questions; each set is aligned to one of the four ladder skills.

For *Jacob's Ladder, Grade 3*, the skills covered by each selection are as follows:

Title	Ladder Skills
Ancient Rome	A, D
The Circle of Life	A, D
Geometry All Around Us	B, C
The Industrial Revolution	B, C
What's the Chance?	C, D
A World of Resources	A, B

Ancient Rome

According to legend, Rome was founded by twin brothers, Romulus and Remus, in 753 B.C.E. Archaeological evidence of Ancient Rome dates to the 8th century B.C.E., somewhere between 800 B.C.E. and 701 B.C.E. (Remember, in B.C.E., the smaller the number, the more recent the date, so 701 B.C.E. is closer to modern day than 800 B.C.E.) For nearly 1,000 years, Rome was the most important, richest, most powerful city in the Western world. During this time, Rome went through several major changes.

Rome began as the Roman Kingdom. It was ruled by a succession of seven kings. Some time between 509 B.C.E. and 501 B.C.E., the last of the seven kings, Tarquin the Proud, was deposed from his throne, which means he was removed from power. With the end of Tarquin the Proud's reign, the Roman Kingdom became the Roman Republic.

The Roman Republic was governed by a senate rather than a monarch or king. The original senate consisted of 100 heads of Roman families. The senate did not have actual lawmaking powers. Rather, it made recommendations to the Plebeian Council, which received its power from the Roman people. Over time, the senate grew in number and in power. By the end of the Roman Republic, there were more than 300 members of the senate. Although they did not have the power to make laws, the senate held remarkable political power. The senate was responsible for sending and receiving ambassadors to foreign lands, appointing managers of public lands, conducting wars, and distributing public funds.

The Roman Republic came to an end when, in the middle of the first century B.C.E., three men formed the First Triumvirate (trahy-**uhm**-ver-it). These three men were Julius Caesar, Pompey the Great (**pom**-pee), and Crassus (**kras**-uhs). They plotted to control the Roman Republic, and their schemes led to civil war. In 44 B.C.E., Julius Caesar was assassinated, or killed, by senators who did not agree with his politics. Eventually, through a series of struggles for power, Augustus, Caesar's designated heir, gained control and became the undisputed ruler of Rome.

With the ascent of Augustus to power, the Roman Republic became the Roman Empire. The Roman Empire extended across most of Europe to the

Mediterranean Sea with a population that exceeded 50 million people. During the "Reign of Five Good Emperors" from 96–180 C.E., the Roman Empire reached its largest landmass of 2 million square miles. Eventually, the Empire became so large that it was nearly impossible for one ruler to maintain control of the entire Empire. In 293 C.E., the Emperor Diocletian (dahy-*uh*-**klee**-sh*uh*n) divided the Roman Empire into an eastern half and a western half. This division became permanent in 330 C.E. after Constantine established Constantinople as the capital of the Eastern Roman Empire. The Western Empire continued to be known as the Roman Empire. The Empire came to a dramatic end in 476 C.E. when Odoacer, a barbarian warlord, killed the last Western Emperor, Romulus Augustulus. Odoacer then made himself king of Italy. The Byzantine Empire in the east came to a less dramatic end in 1453 C.E. when the ruler of the Ottoman Empire, Mehmed II, conquered Constantinople.

Consequences and Implications

A3

What consequences did the Roman Empire experience because of its large size? What were the implications of these consequences? Justify your answer.

Cause and Effect

A2

What caused the Roman Republic to end? Use evidence from the text to support your answer.

Sequencing

A1

Create a timeline of the major events in the history of Ancient Rome.

ANCIENT ROME

Creative Synthesis

D3

Choose an era from Ancient Rome—the Roman Kingdom, the Roman Republic, or the Roman Empire. Imagine you are a Roman citizen during one of these eras. Write a journal entry about what is happening in your city.

Summarizing

D2

In three sentences or fewer, summarize the fall of the Roman Republic and the rise of the Roman Empire.

Paraphrasing

D1

Rewrite the following statement in your own words:

"For nearly 1,000 years, Rome was the most important, richest, most powerful city in the Western world."

The Circle of Life

All animals journey through a predictable life cycle during their life-span. Most animals, except mammals that give birth to live young, begin as eggs. The female of the species lays the eggs, which begins the life cycle of a new animal. Different kinds of animals experience different life cycles. Let's compare the life cycle of amphibians (ām-fíb'ē-ənz) and insects.

Amphibians

Amphibians, such as frogs, live their entire lives near water because they must return to the water to lay their eggs. Amphibians experience a three-stage life cycle. The stages are the egg stage, the larval stage, and the adult stage. The female amphibians lay their eggs directly in the water, thus beginning the egg stage. When the eggs hatch, the larval stage begins as tadpoles emerge with gills for breathing. As amphibians mature, they develop lungs that allow them to breathe outside of the water.

They also begin growing legs and losing their tails. This process is called *metamorphosis* (met-*uh*-**mawr**-*fuh*-sis), which means a complete change in form. During metamorphosis, amphibians change from gill breathers to lung breathers and from plant eaters to meat eaters (think about a frog sitting on the side of a pond catching bugs—meat—with its long, sticky tongue). Some amphibians, such as salamanders and newts, do not undergo metamorphosis. Instead, they spend their entire lives in the larval stage. They do not develop lungs or lose their tails, and they only grow very short legs.

Insects

Winged insects and nonwinged insects experience two different life cycles. Both types of insects begin as eggs. They both have a larval stage, a pupa stage, and a metamorphosis. However, they journey through these stages in different ways.

Nonwinged Insects

Nonwinged insects have a hard outer skeleton called an *exoskeleton* that protects them. Because of this hard outer covering, these insects must grow in stages. The insects eat, grow larger, and then must periodically shed their exoskeleton through a process called *ecdysis* (**ek**-*duh*-sis). Each time the insect sheds its exoskeleton, it is bigger and more mature.

Therefore, metamorphosis—or the complete change from larva to adult insect—happens gradually over time. Scientists have named this gradual change *simple metamorphosis*.

Winged Insects

Winged insects, such as butterflies and ladybugs, experience four distinct life cycle phases. Like most other animals, they begin their lives as eggs. When they hatch, they enter the larval stage. During the larval stage, a butterfly is called a caterpillar and a ladybug is called a Ladybird beetle. The length of the larval stage varies among species, but during this stage the insects eat and grow. Eventually, the larvae are ready to enter the next stage: The larvae become pupae by encasing themselves inside a chrysalis (**kris**-*uh*-lis) or cocoon. While in the chrysalis, the winged insect undergoes a complete transformation and emerges as an adult butterfly or ladybug. The adult winged insect looks completely different than the larva. Scientists have named this complete transformation *complex metamorphosis*.

THE CIRCLE OF LIFE

Consequences and Implications

A3

What are the consequences of an amphibian or an insect reaching the final stage in the life cycle?

Cause and Effect

A2

What causes a nonwinged insect to move to the next stage of simple metamorphosis?

Sequencing

A1

List, in order, the following:
- Stages of an amphibian's life cycle
- Stages of a winged insect's life cycle

D3

Creative Synthesis

Write about the process of metamorphosis from the perspective of an amphibian, a nonwinged insect, or a winged insect.

D2

Summarizing

Describe the life cycle of nonwinged insects versus that of winged insects in three sentences or less.

D1

Paraphrasing

Rewrite this statement in your own words:

"Therefore, metamorphosis—or the complete change from larva to adult insect—happens gradually over time. Scientists have named this gradual change *simple metamorphosis*."

Geometry All Around Us

Have you ever looked around your classroom, your kitchen, or your backyard and noticed all of the geometry around you? Geometry includes all of the many shapes, lines, angles, points, quadrants, square inches, square feet, and square yards that you see every day.

Look around your classroom. How many different shapes can you find? The board at the front of the room is probably a rectangle. Perhaps the table where you sit is a circle. Maybe there is a globe somewhere in your classroom. A globe is a three-dimensional shape called a *sphere*. What about angles? How many angles do you see in your classroom? Perhaps your chair is connected to your desk. Is the seat at a 90-degree, or right, angle? Or, is it slightly tilted back at a 105- or 110-degree angle? Are the corners of the windows right angles?

Now let's think about your house. Your roof may be shaped like a triangle or perhaps a trapezoid. The walls in your house may form straight lines or they may have some angled corners. Do you know how many square feet are in your house? The architect who designed your house and the contractor who built it used geometry to determine how large each room should be, where the exterior and interior walls should go, and how much square footage the finished home should have. Can you think of another way geometry is used in the building of houses? Here's one example: An architect creates a two-dimensional drawing of a house using lines, points, and angles. The architect gives this two-dimensional drawing to the contractor who then transforms it into a three-dimensional building.

Let's think about your yard. Are there flower gardens? How do your parents know how much potting soil or mulch to buy for the flower gardens? They use geometry to figure out the areas of the different flowerbeds. Once they know the square footage of each bed, they know how much dirt or mulch is needed to fill each area. Farmers use this same technique when they are deciding how and where to plant their crops. They use geometry to calculate the area of their fields. In places as large as fields, the area often is referred to as acres. One acre is 4,840 square yards or 43,560 square feet. That's a lot of area!

Geometry also is a big part of activities we do every day. For example, when you are driving somewhere new, how do you know where to go? You might look at a map. When looking at a map, you are using geometry. Maps are made up of quadrants,

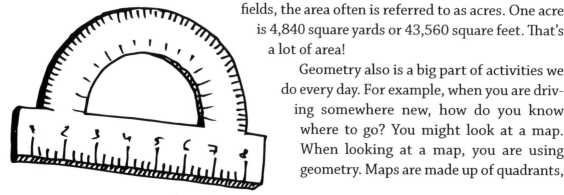

points, and lines. You use the map's key to determine in what quadrant your desired location is; then you follow the lines, or roads, until you reach your destination, which is a point on the map.

Have you ever ridden a skateboard or seen skateboarders riding on ramps? The skateboarders use geometry, even if they don't realize it, when they build their ramps. They must determine the perfect arc for the performance of their tricks. If the arc of the ramp is too steep, they will lose speed and may not make it to the top. However, if the arc of the ramp is too shallow, the skateboarders will not get enough height to perform their tricks. So, the skateboarders must design their ramps with the perfect arc to give them the right amount of speed and the right amount of height.

These are just a few examples of the many different ways geometry is used in everyday life. The next time you are walking down the street, look around you—how many examples of geometry do you see?

Generalizations

B3

Write at least three generalizations about geometry and your everyday life.

Classifications

B2

Study your list from B1. Classify the examples into categories you create. You may not have a "miscellaneous" or "other" category.

Details

B1

Look around you. List as many examples of geometry as you can in 2 minutes. (You should have at least 25 examples.)

GEOMETRY ALL AROUND US

C3 — Main Idea, Theme, or Concept

Main Idea: What is the main idea of "Geometry All Around Us"? Justify your answer.

C2 — Inference

Based on the text, what inferences can you make about the use of geometry?

C1 — Literary Elements

An architect's use of geometry might be characterized as design, and a farmer's use of geometry might be characterized as agricultural. How might a skateboarder's use of geometry be characterized? Use evidence from the text to support your answer.

The Industrial Revolution

The Industrial Revolution began in Great Britain during the late 18th century and early 19th century. During the Revolution, manual labor was replaced by industry, manufacturing, and machinery. There also were dramatic changes in technology, socioeconomics, and culture.

The causes of the Industrial Revolution are still being debated. One theory states that in the 17th century, the borders of Great Britain were better controlled, there was less disease coming into the country from surrounding areas, and more children were living past infancy. All of these conditions led to an increased workforce without enough agricultural work for everyone. Therefore, people began "cottage industries" such as weaving, lace making, and sewing in their homes. Then, in 1700, Jethro Tull invented the seed drill. When farmers used the seed drill, more seeds took root, which led to larger crops, particularly of cotton. As the amount of cotton increased, the demand for products made from cotton also increased. Shortly, the demand for cotton products far exceeded the cottage industries' ability to supply these products. There was a demand for more efficient means of weaving and sewing. According to this theory, then, the Industrial Revolution began in the textile industry to meet the demands of products made from the increased cotton supply.

Another theory cites the expansion of colonial territories, such as America, as the cause of the Industrial Revolution. Expanding territories like America were demanding products from Great Britain. This demand led to the need for more efficient means of production, which then led to the Revolution.

A third theory links the Industrial Revolution to the Scientific Revolution that took place during the 16th century. The Scientific Revolution sparked many inventions, including the steam engine, which made the Industrial Revolution possible.

Although there may be disagreement over the causes of the Industrial Revolution, there certainly is no debate about the many important innovations during this time period, especially in the textile industry. These innovations included the flying shuttle, invented by a watchmaker, which allowed weavers to weave cotton more quickly. Once the

weavers were able to work more quickly, the spinners could not keep up with them. In 1764, James Hargreaves won a contest with his invention, the spinning jenny, which allowed spinners to spin 6–8 threads at once rather than just one thread. Later versions of the spinning jenny could spin as many as 80 threads at once!

In 1769, Richard Arkwright made it possible for spinners to work even faster. He invented the water frame, which used water power to operate spinning wheels, further increasing the speed of the production process. With the water frame, multiple machines could spin at once with just one person overseeing them all; each machine did not need a person operating it. Then, in 1785, Edmund Cartwright patented the power loom, which increased the speed of weaving so the weavers could keep up with the spinners.

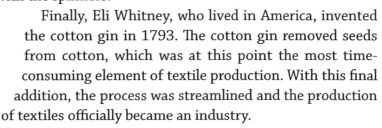

Finally, Eli Whitney, who lived in America, invented the cotton gin in 1793. The cotton gin removed seeds from cotton, which was at this point the most time-consuming element of textile production. With this final addition, the process was streamlined and the production of textiles officially became an industry.

Generalizations

B3

Write at least three generalizations about the Industrial Revolution and how it relates to the modern world.

Classifications

B2

Look at your list from B1. Classify each item on your list into a category. You may not have a "miscellaneous" or "other" category.

Details

B1

List at least 15–20 ways the Industrial Revolution affected the modern world.

THE INDUSTRIAL REVOLUTION

Main Idea, Theme, or Concept

C3

Main Idea: What is the main idea of the selection "The Industrial Revolution?" Write a new title for the selection that better represents its main idea.

Inference

C2

Which of the three theories about the beginning of the Industrial Revolution is best supported by evidence? Explain your answer using details from the text.

Literary Elements

C1

How would you characterize men like Richard Arkwright, Edmund Cartwright, and Eli Whitney? Use details from the text to support your answer.

What's the Chance?

Have you ever tried to determine what your chances were of rolling a 6 with a pair of dice? Or what your chances were of a penny landing on heads versus tails? All of these questions can be answered with a math strategy known as *probability*.

Probability is the measure of how likely an event is to occur based on the number of ways the event could occur and the total number of possible outcomes. Confusing? Let's review some words that are related to probability and then look at an example. Before you can understand probability, you need to know what experiment, outcome, and event mean in relation to it. An *experiment* is a situation that involves chance and leads to outcomes. The result of a single trial is an *outcome*. An *event* is one or more outcomes. OK, now let's look at an example.

Imagine you are rolling a die (that's singular for dice). This is your experiment—you cannot control what number the die will land on, and therefore you are involved in a situation dealing with chance. What is the probability that your die will land on the number 3? Landing on the number 3 would be an outcome or the result of a single trial or roll. How many other possible outcomes are there? Well, you could land on 1, 2, 4, 5, or 6, so there are five other possible outcomes. How many total possible outcomes are there? The total number of possible outcomes is the same as the total of numbers on the die, or six. So, if there is only one outcome that will result in you rolling a 3, and there are six total outcomes, then the chances of you rolling a 3 are 1 in 6 or 1/6. Make sense?

Let's look at another example. Imagine there are four marbles in a bag. One marble is yellow, one is blue, one is green, and one is red. When you pull a marble out of the bag, how many possible outcomes are there? That's right! There are four possible outcomes because there are four different colors. Now, what are your chances of pulling a red marble out of the bag? Only one outcome will lead to a red marble coming out of the bag, so the chances of you drawing a red marble are 1 in 4 or 1/4. The same probability also would apply to the yellow, blue, and green marbles.

Both of these examples are of probability scenarios with equally likely outcomes. When rolling a die, you are equally likely to roll a 4 as you are to roll a 2. When drawing a marble out of the bag, you are equally likely to draw one color as another. Sometimes, though, situations involving probability do not have equally likely outcomes. Probability is considered not equally likely if there is a chance that one outcome will occur more or less frequently than another outcome. For example, imagine you have a bag with six blue candies and three red candies. Are you more likely to draw a blue candy or a red candy? First, let's determine how many total outcomes there are. This number will be the same as the total number of candies, or nine. Now, how many outcomes will result in you pulling a blue candy out of the bag? Six outcomes result in a blue candy, so the probability of you getting a blue candy is 6 out of 9 or 6/9. The chances of you getting a red candy are 3 out of 9 or 3/9 because there are only three red candies. In this example, it is more likely that you will draw a blue candy than a red candy. Therefore, the probability of these events occurring is not equally likely.

C3

Main Idea, Theme, or Concept

Main Idea: What is the main idea of "What's the Chance?"
Use evidence from the text to support your answer.

C2

Inference

If P = probability, A = event A, and B = event B, what inferences
can you make about the following mathematical sentences?

1. $P(A) > P(B)$

2. $P(A) = P(B)$

3. $P(A) < P(B)$

C1

Literary Elements

If probability were a person, what kind of person would
it be? Describe probability. Be sure to include details
from the text to support your description.

Creative Synthesis

D3

Write a math word problem that requires the use of probability to solve.

Summarizing

D2

In three sentences or less, describe the differences between equally likely and not equally likely probability.

Paraphrasing

D1

Rewrite the following statement in your own words:

"Probability is the measure of how likely an event is to occur based on the number of ways the event could occur and the total number of possible outcomes."

A World of Resources

Our world is full of many natural resources that people use each and every day. Some examples of natural resources include air, solar energy, aluminum, natural gas, coal, trees, fish, farm animals, and crops. Natural resources can be classified into three different categories: renewable, flow, and nonrenewable.

Renewable natural resources are living resources like fish, deer, trees, and coffee that can grow back or renew themselves with time. In order for a resource to be renewable, the rate of consumption of the resource cannot exceed the amount of time it takes for the resource to replace itself. Metals are an exception to this rule. Metals cannot renew themselves, but they still are considered renewable resources because they can be recycled and reused. Metals, like the aluminum used for soda cans, are not destroyed during the production cycle. Because they are not destroyed, metals are easily melted down and used again and again.

Flow natural resources also are renewable. Unlike renewable resources, though, flow resources do not require time to replenish themselves. Air, water, wind, tides, and solar energy all are examples of flow resources. There is an endless supply of these types of natural resources.

Nonrenewable natural resources are resources that cannot be remade or regrown. Or, if they can be replenished, they cannot be replenished as quickly as the rate of consumption demands. For example, fossil fuels such as coal, natural gas, and petroleum are nonrenewable resources. Fossil fuels can replenish themselves, but the process takes thousands of years. People cannot wait thousands of years for more coal, natural gas, or petroleum. Therefore, these kinds of natural resources are available in limited quantities and considered nonrenewable.

Another way to classify natural resources is by their matter state. Resources can be solid, liquid, or gas. Examples include trees for solid matter, tides for liquid matter, and air for gas matter.

Natural resources also can be classified as organic or inorganic. Organic natural resources are resources that are living or were once living. Organic resources, such as trees, animals, and crops, can live and die. Any resource containing carbon, a byproduct of living organisms, is considered organic. Inorganic resources are resources that are nonliving, such as rocks, water, and air.

Sometimes, we take natural resources for granted because they are everywhere. We forget how important these natural resources are to the way we live our lives. We must all make an effort to appreciate and protect Earth's natural resources.

Consequences and Implications

A3

What would be the consequences of using all of the Earth's nonrenewable resources? Give an example to explain your answer.

Cause and Effect

A2

What would be the effect of humans consuming, or using, a renewable resource at a faster rate than it can replenish itself? Use evidence from the text to support your answer.

Sequencing

A1

List the order in which classification of natural resources was discussed in the text.

Generalizations

B3

Write at least three generalizations about natural resources based on your list and your classifications.

Classifications

B2

Using the classifications discussed in the text, classify the natural resources on your list.

Details

B1

List as many natural resources as you can think of in 2 minutes. (List at least 25.)

A WORLD OF RESOURCES

APPENDIX

A

Pre- and Postassessments and Exemplars

Appendix A contains the pre- and postassessment readings and answer forms, as well as a rubric for scoring the assessments. The preassessment should be administered before any work with *Jacob's Ladder, Grade 3* is conducted. After all readings and questions have been answered, the postassessment can be given to track student improvement on the ladder skill sets. Included in this appendix are example answers for both the pre- and postassessments. The answers are taken from student responses given during the piloting of this curriculum.

Preassessment

The Fox and the Leopard

(Originally told by Aesop)

The Fox and the Leopard disputed which was the more beautiful of the two. The Leopard exhibited one by one the various spots that decorated his skin. But the Fox, interrupting him, said, "And how much more beautiful than you am I, who am decorated, not in body but in mind."

Preassessment: Questions

Read and answer each question, using evidence from the reading to support your ideas.

1. What do you think would have happened if the Fox looked like the Leopard? Provide evidence from the story to defend your answer.

    _____

    _____

    _____

    _____

    _____

2. What does the Fox mean when he says, "And how much more beautiful than you am I, who am decorated, not in body but in mind"? Provide evidence from the story to defend your answer.

    _____

    _____

    _____

    _____

    _____

Preassessment: Questions, *continued.*

3. What is the moral of this story? Give a reason why you think so.

_____

_____

_____

_____

_____

_____

4. Create a new title for this fable. Give a reason why your title is better than the original title.

_____

_____

_____

_____

_____

_____

Postassessment

The Frogs and the Well

(Originally told by Aesop)

Two frogs lived together in a marsh. But one hot summer the marsh dried up, and they left it to look for another place to live in, for frogs like damp places if they can get them. By and by they came to a deep well, and one of them looked down into it, and said to the other, "This looks a nice cool place. Let us jump in and settle here." But the other, who had a wiser head on his shoulders, replied, "Not so fast, my friend. Supposing this well dried up like the marsh, how should we get out again?"

Postassessment: Questions

Read and answer each question, using evidence from the reading to support your ideas.

1. What do you think would have happened if the frogs jumped in the well? Provide evidence from the story to defend your answer.

   _____

   _____

   _____

   _____

   _____

   _____

2. The wise frog said, "Not so fast, my friend. Supposing this well dried up like the marsh, how should we get out again?" What made this question so important for the frog to ask? Provide evidence from the story to defend your answer.

   _____

   _____

   _____

   _____

   _____

   _____

Postassessment: Questions, *continued*.

3. What is the moral of this story? Give a reason why you think so.

    _____

    _____

    _____

    _____

    _____

    _____

4. Create a new title for this fable. Give a reason why your title is better than the original title.

    _____

    _____

    _____

    _____

    _____

    _____

Assessment Scoring Rubric

Question	Points				
	0	**1**	**2**	**3**	**4**
1 Implications and Consequences (Ladder A)	Provides no response or response is inappropriate to the task demand	Limited, vague, inaccurate; rewords the prompt or copies from text	Response is accurate and makes sense but does not adequately address all components of the question or provide rationale from text	Response is accurate; answers all parts of the question; provides a rationale that justifies answer	Response is well written, specific, insightful; answers all parts of the questions, offers substantial support, and incorporates evidence from the text
2 Inference (Ladder C)	Provides no response or response is inappropriate to the task demand	Limited, vague, inaccurate; rewords the prompt or copies from text	Accurate response but literal interpretation with no support from the text	Interpretive response with limited support from the text	Insightful, interpretive, well-written response with substantial support from the text
3 Theme/ Generalization (Ladders B and C)	Provides no response or response is inappropriate to the task demand	Limited, vague, inaccurate; rewords the prompt or copies from text	Literal description of the story without explaining the theme; no reasons why	Valid, interpretive response with limited reasoning from the text	Insightful, interpretive response with substantial justification or reasoning
4 Creative Synthesis (Ladder D)	Provides no response or response is inappropriate to the task demand	Limited, vague, inaccurate; rewords the prompt or copies from text	Appropriate but literal title with no attempt to support	Interpretive title with limited reasoning or justification	Insightful title, interpretive, and extensive justification or reasoning

Example Answers
Preassessment: The Fox and the Leopard

Note. These answers are based on student responses and teacher ratings from field trials conducted by the Center for Gifted Education. The answers have not been changed from the original student response.

1. What do you think would have happened if the Fox looked like the Leopard? Provide evidence from the story to defend your answer.

   1-point responses might include:

   - They would be friends.
   - The leopard would be really mad.
   - They would both look the same.

   2-point responses might include:

   - I think if the fox looked like the leopard they would fight over whose spots looked better.
   - Then the leopard would have thought he was still the most beautiful.
   - The leopard wouldn't start a fight.

   3-point responses might include:

   - They wouldn't fight anymore because they would look the same.
   - The fox would win because he looks the same and is the smartest.
   - They wouldn't care who was most beautiful, only who was the smartest.

   4-point responses might include:

   - The fox would win the dispute because he is most beautiful with spots decorating his skin and he is smart.
   - They wouldn't have even started fighting because they both had spots decorating their skin so they looked the same.
   - They wouldn't care about being beautiful on the outside anymore. They would only care about who was the most beautiful on the inside in their minds.

2. What does the Fox mean when he says, "And how much more beautiful than you am I, who am decorated, not in body but in mind"? Provide evidence from the story to defend your answer.

1-point responses might include:

- The fox means that the leopard is smarter than him.
- He is decorated in mind but not body.
- The fox was being jealous.

2-point responses might include:

- The fox means he is smarter than leopard.
- He meant he may not be as pretty but he is smarter.
- The fox means that his mind is more beautiful than the leopard.

3-point responses might include:

- He means that the leopard is more pretty on the outside but the fox is more wise.
- The fox meant that the leopard was being selfish and he meant that it does not matter how you look on the outside but what matters is how you act on the inside.
- He meant that it's better to be smart than to be beautiful.

4-point responses might include:

- The fox means he's smart and better than the leopard because he said he was decorated in the mind.
- The fox means he's more beautiful than the fox because he is smarter and that's more important than having pretty spots decorating your skin.
- He means that it's better to be smart than to just be beautiful on the outside. Because he said he is more beautiful because he is decorated "not in body but in mind."

3. What is the moral of this story? Give a reason why you think so.

1-point responses might include:

- It is OK to look better than somebody else.
- The moral is that two animals argue over who is more beautiful.
- The moral of the story is the fox is more beautiful.

2-point responses might include:

- I think the lesson of this story is not to argue over who is more beautiful.
- The lesson is everyone can be beautiful.
- You shouldn't brag about your beauty.

3-point responses might include:

- I think the moral of the story is that it doesn't matter if you don't look good it is more important to be smart.
- The moral teaches that people are not just beautiful on the outside, they are beautiful on the inside too.
- The moral is beauty is only skin deep.

4-point responses might include:

- The moral of the story is that it is more important to be smart than to be pretty. Like when the fox said that he is more beautiful than the leopard because he's decorated in mind.
- The lesson is it is better to be smart and decorated in mind like the fox than to just be pretty like the leopard.
- The moral of the story is that you shouldn't show off how good you look, like when the leopard showed off his spots one by one to the fox. It is more important to be beautiful on the inside.

4. Create a new title for this fable. Give a reason why your title is better than the original title.

1-point responses might include:

- The Leopard and the Fox.
- My title is The Cow and the Chicken because I don't like foxes and leopards.
- The Two Animals.

2-point responses might include:

- <u>The Fox and the Leopard Fighting</u>. I think mine is better because it has more words.
- The Spotted Leopard and the Thoughtful Fox.
- My title is The Smart Fox and the Beautiful Leopard.

3-point responses might include:

- <u>The Argument</u> because the fox and the leopard are arguing.
- <u>The Fox and the Leopard Fight</u>. I think it is better because they are fighting about who is more beautiful.
- <u>Who Is More Beautiful?</u> Because the fox and the leopard are trying to prove who is more beautiful.

4-point responses might include:

- <u>The Inside Counts</u>. I think this is a good title because it's the moral of the story and the fox is right, his brain is better than his body.
- <u>Beauty's Only Skin Deep</u>. This is a better title because it tells the moral of the story. The fox shows that just being beautiful on the outside isn't as good as being beautiful on the inside.
- <u>Beautiful in Mind</u>. This title is good because it shows what the fox said about how being beautiful in mind is better than just having decorated skin.

Example Answers
Postassessment: The Frogs and the Well

Note. These answers are based on student responses and teacher ratings from field trials conducted by the Center for Gifted Education. The answers have not been changed from the original student response.

1. What do you think would have happened if the frogs jumped in the well? Provide evidence from the story to defend your answer.

   1-point responses might include:
   - I think that there could have been a real mean frog in the well.
   - I think the frogs would have gone to look for another home because one frog said, not so fast my friend. Supposing the well was dry like the marsh.
   - I think if they jumped in they would be nice and cool.

   2-point responses might include:
   - If the frogs jumped in the well the frog could die in the well.
   - They might have never gotten out of the well.
   - They would have been stuck in the well forever.

   3-point responses might include:
   - I think the frog would have not been able to get out of the well. My evidence is that the other frog warned them that the well might dry up.
   - If the frogs jumped in the well they would have just realized that when the well dries up they would not be able to get out and they would have no water and they would die.
   - I think the well would have dried up and they would not be able to get out because the wise frog told him this.

   4-point responses might include:
   - If the frogs jumped in the well another hot day might come and dry up the well like the marsh and the frogs wouldn't be able to get out of the well because it's so far down.

- I think if the frogs jumped in the well the two little frogs will get stuck in the well. In the story the wise frog said how would we get out again?

- I think if the frogs would have jumped in the well they really would not have been able to get out because no frog can jump out of such a deep place if the water dried up. My evidence from the story is the first frog said, "Not so fast my friend. Supposing this well dried up like the marsh, how should we get out again?"

2. The wise frog said, "Not so fast, my friend. Supposing this well dried up like the marsh, how should we get out again?" What made this question so important for the frog to ask? Provide evidence from the story to defend your answer.

1-point responses might include:

- It was important that the frog said "Not so fast" because the frog knew that there was something in the well.

- The question is important because the wise frog said it.

- But the other frog who had a wiser head on his shoulders replied not so fast my friend.

2-point responses might include:

- I think that the question was important because it made the not wise frog think a little bit.

- I think he just said it to warn the other frog that said "let's jump in."

- It was so important because it could save the other frogs life.

3-point responses might include:

- It was so important for the wise frog to ask because if they jumped in they could not get out. In the story it said it was a deep well.

- This question was important to the story because the wise frog was actually trying to teach the other frog a lesson.

- It was so important the frog asked it because he did not want to die in the well and that is why the frog asked that important question.

4-point responses might include:

- This was important for the frog to ask because the wise one knew that if they jumped in it could dry up like the marsh and they would not be able to get out. The other one was thinking let's jump in.

- This was so important for the wise frog to ask because it made his friend stop and think before he jumped into the deep well. If he didn't ask they could be stuck in the well forever because it could dry up like the marsh and they couldn't get out again.

- It was important because it made his friend think about how they would get out before they jumped in. If he didn't they could have been stuck in the well if it dried up and never been able to get out again.

3. What is the moral of this story? Give a reason why you think so.

1-point responses might include:

- The frogs had to leave the marsh because it is dried up.

- I think the moral of the story is maybe the wise frog should have jumped in.

- The moral of the story is not to jump into the well.

2-point responses might include:

- The moral of the story is that the frog that was not smart thought that it was smart to move into the well but the other said no, what if it dries up like the marsh did.

- The moral of the story is that if you move out of your house and want a new one you should ask somebody about the house.

- The moral of the story is not to live somewhere if you know it's going to dry up quickly.

3-point responses might include:

- Think before you act.

- You should think twice before you do something.

- The moral of this story is to think before you do stuff, because if you're not careful you could die or get hurt.

4-point responses might include:

- I think the moral of this story is to think before you act, because in the story the marsh dried up from the sun and if they had moved into the well without thinking a hot day could come up again and the sun could dry up the cool water in the well and they would be stuck.

- The moral of this story is think before you act. If the frogs jumped in the well without thinking they would be stuck. The wise frog thought first.

- The lesson of this story is if something looks safe that does not mean it is safe. I think that because the one frog thought that it looked safe but the wise one gave a reason why they should not go in there.

4. Create a new title for this fable. Give a reason why your title is better than the original title.

   1-point responses might include:

   - The Frogs Pond is Dried Up.
   - <u>The Frogs and the Pond</u>. I think this is better.
   - <u>How the Frog Got in the Well</u> because the frog is in the well.

   2-point responses might include:

   - The Two Frogs That Went to a Well.
   - The Frogs, the Marsh, and the Well.
   - I think the title should be <u>Finding a Home</u>.

   3-point responses might include:

   - <u>The Frogs' Problem</u>. I think this title is better than the original because the frogs have a problem in the story.
   - <u>The Foolish Frog</u> is a better title because the frog almost jumped into the well and that would be foolish.
   - I think that the title of this story should be, <u>Think, Think, and Think Before You Do Something</u> because you should always think before you do something.

4-point responses might include:

- The Wise Frog. This would be a good title because if the wise frog would not have said, not so fast my friend, the other frog might have lost his life.

- Think Before You Do Something. That is a better title because the frogs had to stop [and] think before they jumped in the well. If they didn't they could have been stuck in the well.

- I think Be Wise Little Frog should be the title because the one frog wanted to go live in the well but his brother said no because it might dry up and they couldn't get out.

APPENDIX
B

Record-Keeping Forms/Documents

Appendix B contains four record-keeping forms and documents:

- *Brainstorming/Answer Sheet*: This should be given to students for completion after reading a selection so that they may jot ideas or questions about the selection they read prior to participating in discussion. The purpose of this sheet is to capture students' thoughts and ideas generated after individually reading a text. This sheet serves as a guide for student preparedness so that the student is ready to share ideas in group discussion.

- *Assessment/Response Form*: This form may be used by the student as an answer sheet for a given ladder. The student may self-assess his or her work on the ladder in the form of a numerical score. The teacher may also provide a numerical form for feedback. In addition, there is space for both the student and the teacher to write comments about the student's work on the ladder.

- *Reflection Page*: This form may be completed by the student after a group or class discussion on the readings. The reflection page is designed as a metacognitive approach to help students reflect on their strengths and weaknesses and to promote process skills. After discussion, students use the reflection page to record new ideas that were generated by others' comments and ideas.

- *Classroom Diagnostic Form*: This form is for teachers and is designed to aid them in keeping track of the progress and skill mastery of their students. With this chart, teachers can record student progress in relation to each ladder skill within a genre and select additional ladders and readings based on student needs.

Name: _____ Date: _____

Brainstorming/Answer Sheet

Use this form to brainstorm thoughts and ideas about the readings and ladder questions before discussing with a partner.

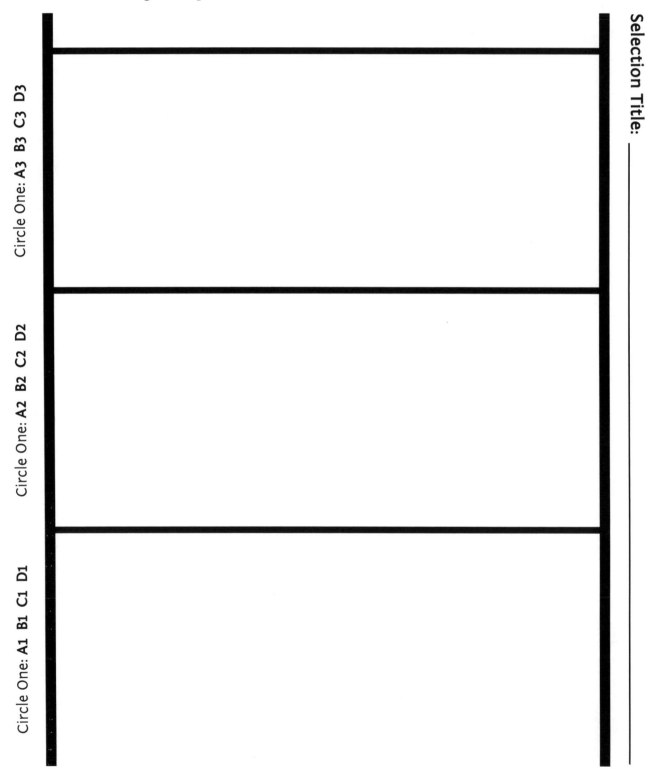

Circle One: **A3 B3 C3 D3**

Circle One: **A2 B2 C2 D2**

Circle One: **A1 B1 C1 D1**

Selection Title: _____

Name: _____ Date: _____

Assessment/Response Form

Use this form as an answer sheet. Both you and your teacher may also assess your work on this page.

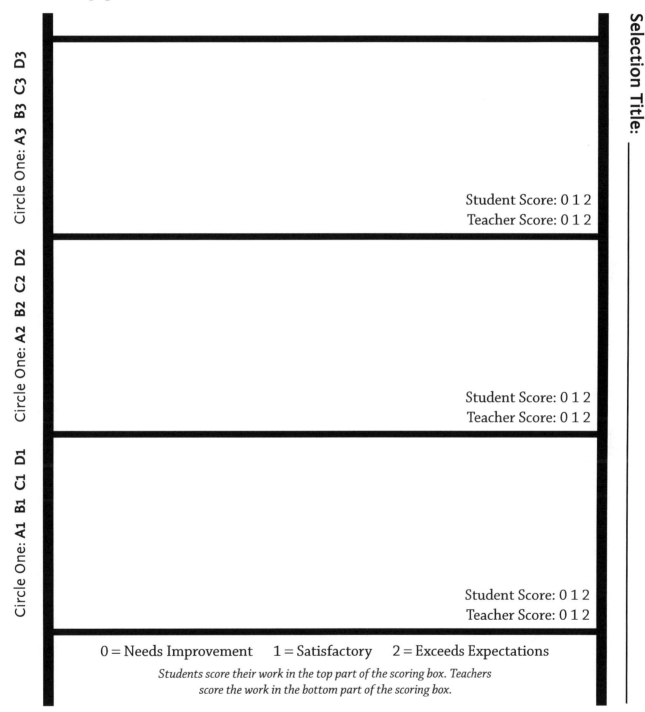

Circle One: **A3 B3 C3 D3**

Selection Title: _____

Student Score: 0 1 2
Teacher Score: 0 1 2

Circle One: **A2 B2 C2 D2**

Student Score: 0 1 2
Teacher Score: 0 1 2

Circle One: **A1 B1 C1 D1**

Student Score: 0 1 2
Teacher Score: 0 1 2

0 = Needs Improvement   1 = Satisfactory   2 = Exceeds Expectations

Students score their work in the top part of the scoring box. Teachers score the work in the bottom part of the scoring box.

Student Comments: Is there anything you would like your teacher to know about your work on this reading?

My Reflection on Today's Reading and Discussion

Selection Title: _____

What I did well:

_____

_____

_____

_____

What I learned:

_____

_____

_____

_____

New ideas I have after discussion:

_____

_____

_____

_____

Next time I need to:

_____

_____

_____

_____

Classroom Diagnostic Form

Short Stories

Use this document to record student completion of ladder sets with the assessment of work.

0 = Needs Improvement   1 = Satisfactory   2 = Exceeds Expectations

Student Name	The Ant and the Dove		The Crow and the Pitcher		Daedalus and Icarus		The Dog and His Reflection		The Fisherman and His Wife
	A	B	A	C	A	C	A	C	A

Classroom Diagnostic Form

Short Stories

Use this document to record student completion of ladder sets with the assessment of work.

0 = Needs Improvement   1 = Satisfactory   2 = Exceeds Expectations

Student Name	How the Camel Got His Hump	The Lion and the Gnat		The Mice in Council		The North Wind and the Sun			Favorite Secret Place	
	A	A	C	A	C	A	A	B	A	C

Classroom Diagnostic Form

Poetry

Use this document to record student completion of ladder sets with the assessment of work.

0 = Needs Improvement   1 = Satisfactory   2 = Exceeds Expectations

Student Name	The Sound of Rain	Winter Shavings	Owl	Fog	Those Days Ago	Summer Song
	C	C	C	B	B	C

Classroom Diagnostic Form

Poetry

Use this document to record student completion of ladder sets with the assessment of work.

0 = Needs Improvement   1 = Satisfactory   2 = Exceeds Expectations

Student Name	Summer in the South A	Dandelions B	Windy Nights A	Aloft C

Classroom Diagnostic Form

Nonfiction

Use this document to record student completion of ladder sets with the assessment of work.

0 = Needs Improvement   1 = Satisfactory   2 = Exceeds Expectations

Student Name	Ancient Rome		The Circle of Life		Geometry All Around Us		The Industrial Revolution		What's the Chance?		A World of Resources	
	A	D	A	D	B	C	B	C	C	D	A	B

Answer Key

This key includes example answers for all ladder questions. Sample answers were generated to illustrate the skills students should be mastering. However, because the questions are open-ended and designed to promote discussion, these answers should only be used as a guide. Variations and original thought should be valued and rewarded.

Short Stories

These are suggested answers only. Answers will vary.

The Ant and the Dove

Ladder Set A

A1. 1. The ant fell in the rapidly moving stream; 2. The dove dropped a leaf into the stream; 3. The ant crawled on the leaf; 4. A hunter took aim at the dove; 5. The ant stung the hunter; 6. The hunter screamed; 7. The dove flew away.

A2.:

Cause	Effect
Ant was thirsty	Went to the stream's edge and fell in
Dove dropped a leaf	The ant was able to get back to shore
Ant stung the hunter	The dove also was able to escape harm

A3. Because the dove was willing to help the ant, the ant later returned the favor. Therefore, the dove saved his own life by dropping the leaf for the ant.

Ladder Set B

B1. Thirsty ant; rapidly moving stream; plucked a leaf; struggling ant; drew his bow; pierced his target; stung him; cried out in pain; dove flew away.

B2.:

Good Turn	Why?
Dove dropped the leaf	Because it gave the ant something to use to float back to shore
Ant stung the hunter	Because the hunter's cry of pain warned the dove who was then able to fly away

B3. Do unto others as you would have them do unto you. OR I'll scratch your back if you'll scratch mine.

The Crow and the Pitcher

Ladder Set A

A1. 1. He put his beak into the pitcher; 2. He tried harder to stick his beak deeper into the pitcher; 3. He dropped pebbles into the pitcher; 4. He saw the water rising and was able to drink it.

A2. The displacement of water by the pebbles caused the water to become available to the crow. The overall effect was that the crow's life was saved.

A3.:

- He would have never gotten to drink any water and he probably would have died of thirst.
- He might have been able to find water somewhere else, but there were no guarantees.
- The water would have spilled and soaked into the ground.
- He might have died of thirst before the rain came.

Ladder Set C

C1. The crow was very creative and persistent. He knew he needed water and he was not willing to give up. He was creative because he figured out how to make the water come to him. Answers for the final question will vary. One example might be: The crow reminds me of the three little pigs. The third little pig decides to build his house out of bricks and works very hard, without giving up, until his house is finished. The three little pigs also are creative because of the way they catch the wolf in the pot at the bottom of the chimney. The crow and the three little pigs are different because the pigs had each other and could develop a plan together. The crow had to save himself all on his own.

C2. Hard work and persistence made the crow successful. His plan worked because he kept adding pebbles until he could see the water. He believed in his plan and persisted even though he did not get immediate results.

C3. The main idea of this story is to never give up. If you work hard enough and think you will succeed, eventually you will.

Daedalus and Icarus

Ladder Set A

A1. 1. Daedalus was given the job of designing a new palace with a secret underground labyrinth for the king of Crete; 2. The king locked Daedalus and Icarus in the highest tower; 3. Daedalus patiently collected bird feathers and old candle wax; 4. Daedalus made two pairs of wings using the feathers and wax; 5. Daedalus told Icarus not to fly too high, and they escaped the palace; 6. Icarus flew too close to the sun, the wax on his wings melted, and he fell to the sea.

A2. Icarus fell into the sea because he did not listen to his father.

A3. This myth reminded me to listen to my parents, especially when safety is concerned. It also should remind society to take the advice of other people who know more about a situation than they do.

Ladder Set C

C1.:

Character	Relationship
Daedalus	Father to Icarus, employee to king of Crete
Icarus	Son of Daedalus
King of Crete	King and the boss of Daedalus and Icarus

The story took place in Ancient Greece on the Island of Crete.

C2. Icarus did not obey his father because he felt such exhilarating freedom while flying. He was so overcome by the desire to fly higher that he forgot about his father's warning.

C3.

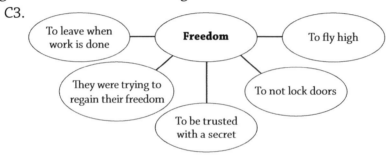

The Dog and His Reflection

Ladder Set A

A1. 1. The butcher throws the dog a bone; 2. The dog sees himself in the water as he is crossing the bridge; 3. He thinks his reflection is another dog with a bigger bone and jumps at it; 4. He almost drowns, but manages to make it to shore; 5. He thinks about the bone he lost and what a silly dog he had been.

A2.:

- The dog lost his bone because he tried to attack the other dog (his own reflection) to get what he thought was a bigger bone.
- The effect of losing his bone was to make the dog realize how foolish and greedy he had been.
- Illustrations will vary. The dog should be happier, even arrogant, in the first picture and sad or self-reproaching in the second drawing.

A3.:
- He lost his bone and nearly drowned.
- He lost his bone, his pride, his arrogance, his greed, his dinner, his spontaneity, and so forth.
- The next time he sees his reflection he will realize it is an image of himself and not another dog.

Ladder Set C

C1.:

Qualities	Positive	Negative
Self-confidence	He feels good about himself	He thought he deserved and could get a bigger, better bone
Greed		He nearly died trying to get a bigger bone
Strength	He was able to save himself from drowning	

C2. I can infer that the dog wanted the bigger bone he thought he saw in the mouth of the other dog. I can also infer that he did not like the idea of another dog having a bigger bone than he had.

C3. The story tells us not to be greedy. We should appreciate what we have, especially when it is enough. We should not want what other people have, but instead should be happy with what we have.

The Fisherman and His Wife

Ladder Set A

A1. 1. The fisherman caught an enchanted fish; 2. The wife told the fisherman he should have asked the fish to grant him a wish; 3. The wife wanted a cottage; 4. The sea was green and yellow; 5. The wife wanted to be emperor; 6. The sea was black and the wind was blowing; 7. The wife was returned to the cottage in which she and the fisherman originally lived.

A2. Every time the wife wished for something else, the fisherman would agree to ask the fish. But every time he came back from getting her wish granted, his wife still was not happy. Every time he got one of her wishes granted, she would immediately want something else.

A3. Because the wife was never satisfied with what she had, she eventually had nothing at all.

How the Camel Got His Hump

Ladder Set A

A1. 1. The Camel ate sticks and thorns and answered anyone who spoke to him with "Humph!"; 2. The Dog asked the Camel to help with the work; 3. Man called the Horse and the Dog and the Ox together to talk about their work; 4. The Djinn stopped to talk with the Horse and the Dog and the Ox; 5. The Camel sat idly in the desert and looked at his reflection in a pool of water; 6. The Djinn tried to get the camel to work; 7. The Camel said "Humph" too many times and a hump grew on his back.

A2. The Man told the Horse and the Dog and the Ox that they would have to work double-time to make up for the work that the Camel didn't do. This made them very angry.

A3. The Camel would be able to work for three days without eating.

The Lion and the Gnat

Ladder Set A

A1. Drawings will vary.

A2. The gnat, the small character, got caught in the spider web because he was preoccupied with wanting to tell the whole world that he had defeated the lion.

A3.:

- One of the consequences of being smaller than other creatures is that you feel like you need to prove yourself to the bigger creatures by trying to beat them.
- One of the consequences of being larger than other creatures makes you think you cannot be defeated by creatures smaller than you.
- One of the consequences of being clever is that you often can outsmart other people, but also can get too carried away by outsmarting them.
- One of the consequences of being too proud is that you forget to look out for yourself and others; you think you are so perfect that you cannot make any mistakes.

Ladder Set C

C1.:

Characters	Similarities	Differences
Lion	Pride; gets defeated; thinks he is better than the other	Lion is big, gets defeated by the gnat
Gnat	Pride; gets defeated; thinks he is better than the other	Gnat is small, gets defeated by the spider

C2. I can tell the gnat was proud because he told the lion he was not afraid of him. I also know he was proud because he flew away quickly to tell everyone that he had defeated the lion.

C3. The main idea of the story is that you should be kind to others and you should not take pride in defeating others. (Stories will vary.)

The Mice in Council

Ladder Set A

A1. 1. Wait until the cat is asleep; 2. Tiptoe out of the mouse hole; 3. Carefully place the bell on a string around the cat's neck; 4. Run as fast as they can back into the mouse hole.

A2.:

In the story, the cat *caused*:	The *effect* was that the mice:
The mice to be scared	Wanted to get rid of the cat
The mice to develop ideas for getting rid of the cat	One mouse suggested putting a bell around the cat's neck

A3. Older is wiser. (The older mouse was the wise one who warned against the dangers of trying to put a bell around the cat's neck.)

Ladder Set C

C1.:

	Qualities	Habits
Cats	Hunters	They like to chase and catch mice
Mice	Scavengers	They like to scuttle around looking for crumbs and cheese

C2. Although putting a bell around the cat's neck would allow the mice to know when the cat was coming, it also would mean that a mouse would have to get very close to the cat. The mouse who took on this job could very easily be caught. So, the question is asking whether or not there is a mouse that would be willing to sacrifice himself for the good of the other mice.

C3. This story teaches us that by working together groups can develop solutions for problems. It also reminds us that sometimes a member of a group has to take chances in order to benefit the entire group.

The North Wind and the Sun

Ladder Set A

A1. The first time the wind blew the man wrapped his coat around himself. The second time the wind blew the man held his coat more tightly around himself.

A2. The effect of the wind blowing more forcefully on the traveler was that the traveler pulled his coat more tightly around him instead of taking it off as the wind had wanted.

A3. The wind tried to use force to blow the man's coat off. Instead, the sun made it seem as if it was the man's decision to take off his coat because he was feeling too warm. The sun's method was better because the decision was placed in the hands of the man—he was not being forced to do something that he may not want to do.

The wind could have blown more gently and made the man think that a nice, pleasant breeze was blowing. Then, the man might have taken off his coat to enjoy the wind's soft caress.

Ladder Set B

B1.:
- The strength of the wind was his great power and force.
- The strength of the sun was her intense heat and awesome light.
- The sun was stronger because she chose to use her power in cooperation with the man's desires rather than trying to use her power to force the man to take off his coat.

B2. Answers will vary, but should include specific examples from students' personal experience and/or texts they have read.

B3. It is easier to convince someone using persuasion than power. Power only goes as far as you can force it. Persuasion works in favor of everyone involved.

Favorite Secret Place

Ladder Set A

A1. 1. The narrator looked up at the clouds in the sky; 2. The narrator let her hand dangle in the water; 3. The narrator plunged her head into the water; 4. The narrator jumped into the water from the top of the mini waterfall.

A2. Plunging her face into the water made her face freeze. She had to bring her face out of the water because it was freezing. She gasped for air because it was so cold. (Stories of own experiences will vary. Comparisons should be between the narrator's reactions and the student's reactions.)

A3. If the narrator did not appreciate nature, she might have been noisy and disturbed the animals and plants around her. This would have changed the story because she would not have talked about the secret of the place and how the birds wanted to be hidden.

Ladder Set C

C1. Sample responses: The narrator includes phrases like:
- "a river, gently lapping at my rock"
- "there is a wide strip of sand, like a very, very small beach"
- "the icy coldness rushing past my fingertips as they become numb"
- "sweat tricking down the side of my face"

C2. Sample responses:
- The narrator says: "Next to me is a river, lapping gently at my rock, which I am sitting upon like a queen of the water."
- The narrator says: "I respect that, the secret. The privacy. I understand and feel nature's presence."
- The narrator says: "It makes me feel special, yet not worthy, that I witnessed the beautifully magnificent moment."
- The narrator says: "I feel at peace, calm, in this beautiful scene of wilderness."

C3. We should appreciate the beauty of nature.

Poetry

These are suggested answers only. Answers will vary.

The Sound of Rain

Ladder Set C

C1. The tone of the poem indicates that the author sees the action of rain in a different way. These are some of the words she uses that show that: "a musical rhythm," "reflecting my image," and "slowly dripping."

C2. The phrases that tell me that the author seems to be outside during a storm are: "mad, ferocious clouds of black and grey;" "drop falls, then another, another, again and again;" "wind whistles and winds around me."

C3. The main idea is that it is a joy to be in the presence of rain.

Winter Shavings

Ladder Set C

C1.:

- Phrases or words: "small and naïve child;" "falling, spiraling;" "already frozen."
- The author uses words and phrases to put pictures in my head by describing what snow looks like and how it moves.
- Illustrations will vary.

C2. By this title, the author is using figurative language to describe snow as "winter shavings," which are really snowflakes. It can be inferred that the snowflakes are light and in small pieces, like shavings of something.

C3.The title, "Winter Shavings," gives the reader a clue about the main idea of the poem because it describes the topic of the poem (snow) using figurative language. The author describes snow and how it moves in this poem. Therefore, the poem is named after the main topic in the poem and the topic is the main idea of the poem.

Owl

Ladder Set C

C1. "Ancient song;" "dripping like velvety paint;" "blanket of soft, heavy sound"

C2. The evidence that is important for indicating that the animal being described is an owl are phrases the author uses like: "last of the animals"; "slips silently into crevices"; and "an ancient song."

C3. Poems will vary.

Fog

Ladder Set B

B1. Illustrations will vary.

B2. Little feet; stealth; cats are very quiet; pouncing; stalking; lingering and watching.

B3. Poems will vary. Students do not necessarily have to choose a pair in the same row. For example, they may choose "wind" and "horse" or "fire" and "bird."

Those Days Ago

Ladder Set B

B1. Pictures may vary, but they must be related to an image from the poem, such as waves crashing, sandcastles standing on the beach, seaweed, the ocean, or the heat of the sand.

Lists will vary. Images should not be redundant; each image should be unique. (If your students have not seen the beach in person, you may want to provide pictures or videos to assist them in completing this activity.)

B2. The images should be categorized by similar features. For example, if a student listed crabs, fish, and starfish, he or she may put these images into a category called Animals Found at the Beach.

B3.:

Generalization	Evidence From the Poem	Evidence From My List
Many items are found at the beach that are not found elsewhere. (Students should list at least four generalizations.)	Seaweed	Starfish

Summer Song

Ladder Set C

C1. Personification is used in this poem. The moon exhibits human qualities because it wanders and has a smile. These are all human characteristics.

C2. The poet implies that the summer moon is different because it is a traveler. The phrases that support my inferences are when the poet writes that the moon has a "faintly ironical smile" and a "detached sleepily indifferent smile."

C3. The main idea of this poem is that the moon is like a traveler because of its movement.

Summer in the South

Ladder Set A

A1. The poem begins with animals and plants starting to appear at the beginning of the summer. Then, the rain comes, followed by sunshine. Because of the rain and the sun, everything in nature grows or becomes active:

Oriole is waiting → rosebuds start to appear → rain comes down → plants begin to sprout → sun shines and plants grow → rain causes the streams to flow → the woods are active with life

A2. Summer changes things in nature because the warm weather causes things to grow and thrive. I know because the poet describes different things that happen in the summer. For example, he says that "the rosebuds peep from their hoods of green, Timid and hesitating."

The change in the streams is because of summer rains. The rain allows plants to grow and causes the streams to flow.

A3. If the seasons never changed, we would not get variety in nature. If it were always summer, people would always be hot, they would never get to see snow, and their grass would always need watering (so the water bill would be very expensive). If it were always winter, people might not be able to spend time outside, plants would never grow, and they would have to run the heater all of the time.

The poem implies that summer is a good time for nature. Plants are starting to grow because the poet says that the garden thrives. The poet describes laughing streams, a smiling sun, and woods running mad with riot. These are all things that make it sound like summer is a good time for nature.

Dandelions

Ladder Set B

B1. Answers will vary, but students must support their answers with words and phrases from the text of the poem.

B2. Examples of positive words/phrases:
- "kind"
- "caring"
- "good friend"
- "it's not what's on the outside but the inside that matters."

Examples of negative words/phrases:
- "not one of them"
- "will not accept me"
- "excluded"
- "ignored and overlooked"
- "inferior background"
- "not popular"

Windy Nights

Ladder Set A

A1. "Whenever," "gallop," and "by." These words are important to the order of the poem because "whenever" tells you when the man rides his horse, "gallop" tells you how he rides his horse, and "by" tells in what direction and in what pattern he rides his horse. All of these words combined give an image of the sequence of events that occur when the man decides to ride.

A2. The wind causes the man to ride when it is high. It also causes the trees to cry aloud and the ships to be tossed at sea. Other effects that the wind might cause include a howling sound as it moves between buildings, for rain to fall sideways, for sand to be blown about, and leaves to be churned up.

A3. He is the wind being personified by a man riding the horse. Line 4 reads, "A man goes riding by." The lines later in the poem that use the word "he" are referring to the galloping nature of the blowing wind.

Aloft

Ladder Set C

C1. The metaphor is "Our seabird is the truest ship . . ." The author compares the seabird to a ship. She also says that the seabird: "floats on the skies"; "has feathery sails"; "has a light keel bone"; "has a tail like a rudder"; "is friends with the wind"; "perches in port"; and "carries the ocean's song."

The two similes are "his tail as a rudder" and "swift as a current."

C2. The evidence from the poem that suggests that the author sees the seabird as a graceful animal are the poet's use of the phrases "with feathery sails," "friends with the wind," and "carries the ocean's song."

C3. The main idea of this poem is that a seabird is like a sailing ship.

Nonfiction

These are suggested answers only. Answers will vary.

Ancient Rome

Ladder Set A

A1. 753 B.C.E., Romulus and Remus founded Rome (or archaeological evidence dates the beginning of Rome to the 8th century B.C.E.); between 509 and 501 B.C.E. the Roman Kingdom became the Roman Republic; in 44 B.C.E. Julius Caesar was assassinated; Augustus came to power in 31 B.C.E., beginning the Roman Empire; 96–180 C.E., Roman Empire reached its largest landmass; 293 C.E., Emperor Diocletian split the Empire into eastern and western halves; 330 C.E., Constantine made Constantinople the capital of the Eastern Empire (Byzantine Empire); 476 C.E., the Western Roman Empire fell to Odoacer, who killed the Emperor, Romulus Augustulus, and proclaimed himself king of Italy; 1453 C.E., Byzantine Empire fell to the Ottoman Empire or Mehmed II.

A2. Answers will vary. Some possible responses: Civil war; the senate gained too much power and was no longer representing the people; the government was corrupt; the rebellion of the First Triumvirate.

A3. Because of its large size, the Roman Empire could not be controlled by one ruler. The consequences, therefore, were that the Empire was split in half. Because of the split, the Eastern Empire became a different Empire all together. Not long after the split became official with the naming as Constantinople as the capital of the Eastern Empire, the Western Empire was conquered by Germanic Tribes.

Ladder Set D

D1. Answers will vary. Students must rewrite the statement, not just change a few words.

D2. Answers will vary. Students should include the excessive power of the senate, the rebellion of the First Triumvirate, and the rise of Augustus after many internal struggles for power. Ensure students' answers are three sentences or less and encompass the main ideas of the fall of the Roman Republic and the subsequent rise of the Roman Empire.

D3. Answers will vary. Check students' answers to ensure that the journal entry includes events that are likely to have happened during the era chosen.

The Circle of Life

Ladder Set A

A1. Amphibian: egg, larvae, adult; winged insect: egg, larvae, pupae, adult.

A2. The nonwinged insects move to the next stage of development when they shed their exoskeleton. They shed their exoskeleton when they have become too large for it.

A3. Once an amphibian or an insect reaches the final stage of the life cycle, the new adult has the responsibility to continue the life cycle. The adult amphibian or insect must lay eggs to begin the life cycle over again. In order to have this opportunity, it must protect itself, find food to eat, and so forth.

Ladder Set D

D1. Answers will vary. Students must rewrite the statement, not just change a few words.

D2. Answers will vary. Students should mention simple metamorphosis versus complex metamorphosis. They also may mention that winged insects have a distinct pupae stage whereas nonwinged insects do not. Make sure student answers are three sentences or less and encompass the main differences between the two types of insects.

D3. Answers will vary. Student accounts of the amphibian's or insect's experience should be accurate. For example, if a student decides to write about the experience from a salamander's perspective, the salamander should not advance beyond the larval stage of development.

Geometry All Around Us

Ladder Set B

B1. Answers will vary. Check students' lists to ensure they include only examples of geometry.

B2. Answers will vary based on what students have included on their lists. Check their classification using the definitions and descriptions included in the text, as well as the definitions of geometrical terms.

B3. Answers will vary. Generalizations should be broad, overarching statements that apply to geometry and its everyday uses.

Ladder Set C

C1. Answers will vary. Some possible responses include recreational, entertainment, sports, and so forth.

C2. Answers will vary. Students should mention that the inference can be made that geometry is very important to the world as we know it. Without geometry, houses might not be symmetrical, farmers might buy too many or too few seeds for their crops, and/or skateboarders may not be able to perform many of their most impressive tricks.

C3. Answers will vary. Students should focus on the prevalence of geometry in the things we see and do every day.

The Industrial Revolution

Ladder Set B

B1. Answers will vary. Depending on the amount of students' prior knowledge, some examples may not be found in the text. Check students' answers to ensure they are related to advances made during the Industrial Revolution.

B2. Answers will vary based on what students have included on their lists. Check that their classifications and categories are logical and appropriately organized.

B3. Answers will vary. Generalizations should be broad, overarching statements that apply to the Industrial Revolution and its impact on our modern world.

Ladder Set C

C1. Answers will vary. Possible answers might include characteristics such as inventive, creative, forward thinking, ahead of their time, intelligent, productive, contributors to the advancement of technology, and so forth.

C2. Answers will vary. Check students' answers for logical support based on the information in the text and, possibly, previous knowledge of the Industrial Revolution.

C3. Answers will vary. Check students' answers for justification related to the details in the text.

What's the Chance?

Ladder Set C

C1. Answers will vary but would include how certain things people do are predictable, but people cannot control what happens. They also may describe how people plan events but can't control the outcomes.

C2. $P(A) > P(B)$: The probability of event A occurring is greater than the probability of event B occurring; $P(A) = P(B)$: Events A and B are equally likely to occur; $P(A) < P(B)$: The probability of event A occurring is less than the probability of event B occurring.

C3. Answers will vary. Answers should mention that chance can be mathematically predicted through probability. They also should mention equally likely versus not equally likely probability.

Ladder Set D

D1. Answers will vary. Students must rewrite the statement, not just change a few words.

D2. Answers will vary. Students should mention that equally likely probability means that the chances of one outcome occurring are equal to the chances of another outcome. Not equally likely probability means that the chances of one outcome occurring are greater or less than the chances of another outcome. Ensure students' answers are three sentences or less and encompass the main differences between the two types of probability.

D3. Answers will vary. Check students' answers to ensure that the word problem requires probability and uses probability correctly.

A World of Resources

Ladder Set A

A1. Renewable, flow, nonrenewable; answer also may include: states of matter (solid, liquid, gas), organic, inorganic.

A2. Answers will vary. Students should indicate that once a renewable resource is used, it begins to replenish itself. However, if the rate of consumption exceeds the rate of renewal, then we will be in danger of depleting the supply of resources.

A3. Answers will vary. Students should indicate that once a nonrenewable resource is gone, it cannot be replenished, or at least not quickly. They also should indicate that people will have to find alternative resources if they exhaust the supply of nonrenewable resources. Some students may mention nonrenewable resources such as gas; if we run out, then we will not be able to use our cars until we find an alternative fuel.

Ladder Set B

B1. Answers will vary. Check students' list to ensure they include only natural resources or that students have indicated how an item on their list is derived from a natural resource.

B2. Answers will vary based on what students have included on their lists. Check their classification using the definitions and descriptions included in the text.

B3. Answers will vary. Generalizations should be broad, overarching statements that apply to all natural resources or to a specific category of natural resources.

Common Core State Standards Alignment

Cluster	Common Core State Standards in ELA-Literacy
College and Career Readiness Anchor Standards for Reading	CCRA.R.1 Read closely to determine what the text says explicitly and to make logical inferences from it; cite specific textual evidence when writing or speaking to support conclusions drawn from the text. (Short Stories: Ladders A, B, C) (Poetry: Ladders A, B, C) (Nonfiction: Ladders A, B, C, D)
	CCRA.R.2 Determine central ideas or themes of a text and analyze their development; summarize the key supporting details and ideas. (Short Stories: Ladders A, C) (Poetry: Ladder C) (Nonfiction: Ladder C)
	CCRA.R.3 Analyze how and why individuals, events, or ideas develop and interact over the course of a text. (Short Stories: Ladders A, B, C) (Poetry: Ladders A, B) (Nonfiction: Ladders A, B)
	CCRA.R.4 Interpret words and phrases as they are used in a text, including determining technical, connotative, and figurative meanings, and analyze how specific word choices shape meaning or tone. (Poetry: Ladder A)
	CCRA.R.10 Read and comprehend complex literary and informational texts independently and proficiently. (Short Stories: Ladder B) (Poetry: Ladder B) (Nonfiction: Ladders A, B)
College and Career Readiness Anchor Standards for Writing	CCRA.W.2 Write informative/explanatory texts to examine and convey complex ideas and information clearly and accurately through the effective selection, organization, and analysis of content. (Short Stories: Ladder B) (Poetry: Ladder B) (Nonfiction: Ladders A, B, D)

Cluster	Common Core State Standards in ELA-Literacy
College and Career Readiness Anchor Standards for Writing, *continued*	CCRA.W.3 Write narratives to develop real or imagined experiences or events using effective technique, well-chosen details and well-structured event sequences. (Poetry: Ladder A) (Nonfiction: Ladder D)
	CCRA.W.9 Draw evidence from literary or informational texts to support analysis, reflection, and research. (Poetry: Ladder C) (Nonfiction: Ladders C, D)
College and Career Readiness Anchor Standards for Speaking and Listening	CCRA.SL.1 Prepare for and participate effectively in a range of conversations and collaborations with diverse partners, building on others' ideas and expressing their own clearly and persuasively. (Short Stories: Ladders A, B) (Poetry: Ladders A, B, C) (Nonfiction: Ladders A, B, C, D)
	CCRA.SL.4 Present information, findings, and supporting evidence such that listeners can follow the line of reasoning and the organization, development, and style are appropriate to task, purpose, and audience. (Short Stories: Ladder B) (Poetry: Ladders B, C) (Nonfiction: Ladders A, B, C, D)
College and Career Readiness Anchor Standards for Language	CCRA.L.1 Demonstrate command of the conventions of standard English grammar and usage when writing or speaking. (Short Stories: Ladder B) (Poetry: Ladders B, C) (Nonfiction: Ladders A, B, C, D)
	CCRA.L.5 Demonstrate understanding of figurative language, word relationships, and nuances in word meanings. (Poetry: Ladder A)
Reading: Literature, Grade 3	RL.3.1 Ask and answer questions to demonstrate understanding of a text, referring explicitly to the text as the basis for the answers. (Short Stories: Ladders A, B, C) (Poetry: Ladders A, B, C)
	RL.3.2 Recount stories, including fables, folktales, and myths from diverse cultures; determine the central message, lesson, or moral and explain how it is conveyed through key details in the text. (Short Stories: Ladders A, B, C) (Poetry: Ladders B, C)
	RL.3.3 Describe characters in a story (e.g., their traits, motivations, or feelings) and explain how their actions contribute to the sequence of events. (Short Stories: Ladders A, C) (Poetry: Ladder A)
	RL.3.4 Determine the meaning of words and phrases as they are used in a text, distinguishing literal from nonliteral language. (Poetry: Ladders B, C)
	RL.3.5 Refer to parts of stories, dramas, and poems when writing or speaking about a text, using terms such as chapter, scene, and stanza; describe how each successive part builds on earlier sections. (Short Stories: Ladder A) (Poetry: Ladder A)

Cluster	Common Core State Standards in ELA-Literacy
Reading: Literature, Grade 3, *continued*	RL.3.10 By the end of the year, read and comprehend literature, including stories, dramas, and poetry, at the high end of the grades 2–3 text complexity band independently and proficiently. (Short Stories: Ladders A, C) (Poetry: Ladder A)
Reading: Literature, Grade 4	RL.4.1 Refer to details and examples in a text when explaining what the text says explicitly and when drawing inferences from the text. (Short Stories: Ladders A, B) (Poetry: Ladders A, B, C)
	RL.4.2 Determine a theme of a story, drama, or poem from details in the text; summarize the text. (Short Stories: Ladder C) (Poetry: Ladders B, C)
	RL.4.3 Describe in depth a character, setting, or event in a story or drama, drawing on specific details in the text (e.g., a character's thoughts, words, or actions). (Short Stories: Ladders A, B, C) (Poetry: Ladder A)
	RL.4.4 Determine the meaning of words and phrases as they are used in a text, including those that allude to significant characters found in mythology (e.g., Herculean). (Poetry: Ladders B, C)
	RL.4.9 Compare and contrast the treatment of similar themes and topics (e.g., opposition of good and evil) and patterns of events (e.g., the quest) in stories, myths, and traditional literature from different cultures. (Short Stories: Ladders B, C)
	RL.4.10 By the end of the year, read and comprehend literature, including stories, dramas, and poetry, in the grades 4–5 text complexity band proficiently, with scaffolding as needed at the high end of the range. (Short Stories: Ladders A, C) (Poetry: Ladder A)
Reading: Literature, Grade 5	RL.5.1 Quote accurately from a text when explaining what the text says explicitly and when drawing inferences from the text. (Short Stories: Ladders A, B, C) (Poetry: Ladders A, B, C)
	RL.5.2 Determine a theme of a story, drama, or poem from details in the text, including how characters in a story or drama respond to challenges or how the speaker in a poem reflects upon a topic; summarize the text. (Short Stories: Ladders A, B, C) (Poetry: Ladders B, C)
	RL.5.3 Compare and contrast two or more characters, settings, or events in a story or drama, drawing on specific details in the text (e.g., how characters interact). (Short Stories: Ladders A, B, C) (Poetry: Ladder A)
	RL.5.4 Determine the meaning of words and phrases as they are used in a text, including figurative language such as metaphors and similes. (Poetry: Ladders B, C)

Cluster	Common Core State Standards in ELA-Literacy
Reading: Literature, Grade 5, *continued*	RL.5.5 Explain how a series of chapters, scenes, or stanzas fits together to provide the overall structure of a particular story, drama, or poem. (Short Stories: Ladder A)
	RL.5.9 Compare and contrast stories in the same genre (e.g., mysteries and adventure stories) on their approaches to similar themes and topics. (Short Stories: Ladder C)
	RL.5.10 By the end of the year, read and comprehend literature, including stories, dramas, and poetry, at the high end of the grades 4–5 text complexity band independently and proficiently. (Short Stories: Ladder C) (Poetry: Ladder A)
Reading: Informational Text: Grade 3	RI.3.1 Ask and answer questions to demonstrate understanding of a text, referring explicitly to the text as the basis for the answers. (Nonfiction: Ladders A, D)
	RI.3.3 Describe the relationship between a series of historical events, scientific ideas or concepts, or steps in technical procedures in a text, using language that pertains to time, sequence, and cause/effect. (Nonfiction: Ladders A, D)
Reading: Informational Text: Grade 4	RI.4.1 Refer to details and examples in a text when explaining what the text says explicitly and when drawing inferences from the text. (Nonfiction: Ladders A, D)
	RI.4.2 Determine the main idea of a text and explain how it is supported by key details; summarize the text. (Nonfiction: Ladder D)
	RI.4.3 Explain events, procedures, ideas, or concepts in a historical, scientific, or technical text, including what happened and why, based on specific information in the text. (Nonfiction: Ladder A)
Reading: Informational Text: Grade 5	RI.5.1 Quote accurately from a text when explaining what the text says explicitly and when drawing inferences from the text. (Nonfiction: Ladders A, D)
	RI.5.3 Explain the relationships or interactions between two or more individuals, events, ideas, or concepts in a historical, scientific, or technical text based on specific information in the text. (Nonfiction: Ladder A)
	RI.5.6 Analyze multiple accounts of the same event or topic, noting important similarities and differences in the point of view they represent. (Nonfiction: Ladder D)
Writing, Grade 3	W.3.3 Write narratives to develop real or imagined experiences or events using effective technique, descriptive details, and clear event sequences. (Short Stories: Ladder C) (Poetry: Ladder A) (Nonfiction: Ladder D)

Cluster	Common Core State Standards in ELA-Literacy
Writing, Grade 3, *continued*	W.3.8 Recall information from experiences or gather information from print and digital sources; take brief notes on sources and sort evidence into provided categories. (Short Stories: Ladders B, C) (Poetry: Ladders A, B, C) (Nonfiction: Ladders A, B, C)
Writing, Grade 4	W.4.3 Write narratives to develop real or imagined experiences or events using effective technique, descriptive details, and clear event sequences. (Short Stories: Ladder C) (Poetry: Ladder A) (Nonfiction: Ladder D)
	W.4.8 Recall relevant information from experiences or gather relevant information from print and digital sources; take notes and categorize information, and provide a list of sources. (Short Stories: Ladder B) (Poetry: Ladders B, C) (Nonfiction: Ladders A, B, C)
Writing, Grade 5	W.5.3 Write narratives to develop real or imagined experiences or events using effective technique, descriptive details, and clear event sequences. (Short Stories: Ladder C) (Poetry: Ladder A) (Nonfiction: Ladder D)
	W.5.8 Recall relevant information from experiences or gather relevant information from print and digital sources; summarize or paraphrase information in notes and finished work, and provide a list of sources. (Short Stories: Ladder B) (Poetry: Ladders B, C) (Nonfiction: Ladders A, B, C)
Speaking and Listening, Grade 3	SL.3.1 Engage effectively in a range of collaborative discussions (one-on-one, in groups, and teacher-led) with diverse partners on grade 3 topics and texts, building on others' ideas and expressing their own clearly. (Short Stories: Ladders A, B, C) (Poetry: Ladders A, B, C) (Nonfiction: Ladders A, B, C, D)
	SL.3.2 Determine the main ideas and supporting details of a text read aloud or information presented in diverse media and formats, including visually, quantitatively, and orally. (Poetry: Ladder C) (Nonfiction: Ladder C)
	SL.3.3 Ask and answer questions about information from a speaker, offering appropriate elaboration and detail. (Short Stories: Ladders B, C) (Poetry: Ladders B, C) (Nonfiction: Ladders A, B, C)
	SL.3.4 Report on a topic or text, tell a story, or recount an experience with appropriate facts and relevant, descriptive details, speaking clearly at an understandable pace. (Short Stories: Ladders A, B, C) (Poetry: Ladders A, B, C) (Nonfiction: Ladders A, B, C, D)

Cluster	Common Core State Standards in ELA-Literacy
Speaking and Listening, Grade 3, *continued*	SL.3.6 Speak in complete sentences when appropriate to task and situation in order to provide requested detail or clarification. (See grade 3 Language standards 1 and 3 here for specific expectations.) (Short Stories: Ladders A, B, C) (Poetry: Ladders A, B, C) (Nonfiction: Ladders A, B, C)
Speaking and Listening, Grade 4	SL.4.1 Engage effectively in a range of collaborative discussions (one-on-one, in groups, and teacher-led) with diverse partners on grade 4 topics and texts, building on others' ideas and expressing their own clearly. (Short Stories: Ladders A, B, C) (Poetry: Ladders A, B, C) (Nonfiction: Ladders A, B, C)
	SL.4.2 Paraphrase portions of a text read aloud or information presented in diverse media and formats, including visually, quantitatively, and orally. (Nonfiction: Ladder D)
	SL.4.4 Report on a topic or text, tell a story, or recount an experience in an organized manner, using appropriate facts and relevant, descriptive details to support main ideas or themes; speak clearly at an understandable pace. (Nonfiction: Ladder D)
Speaking and Listening, Grade 5	SL.5.1 Engage effectively in a range of collaborative discussions (one-on-one, in groups, and teacher-led) with diverse partners on grade 5 topics and texts, building on others' ideas and expressing their own clearly. (Short Stories: Ladders A, B, C) (Poetry: Ladders A, B, C) (Nonfiction: Ladders A, B, C, D)
	SL.5.2 Summarize a written text read aloud or information presented in diverse media and formats, including visually, quantitatively, and orally. (Short Stories: Ladder A) (Poetry: Ladders B, C)
	SL.5.4 Report on a topic or text or present an opinion, sequencing ideas logically and using appropriate facts and relevant, descriptive details to support main ideas or themes; speak clearly at an understandable pace. (Short Stories: Ladders A, C) (Poetry: Ladder A) (Nonfiction: Ladder D)
Language, Grade 3	L.3.1 Demonstrate command of the conventions of standard English grammar and usage when writing or speaking. (Short Stories: Ladders A, B) (Poetry: Ladders A, B, C) (Nonfiction: Ladders A, B, C, D)
	L.3.3 Use knowledge of language and its conventions when writing, speaking, reading, or listening. (Short Stories: Ladders A, B) (Poetry: Ladders A, B, C) (Nonfiction: Ladders A, B, C, D)
	L.3.6 Acquire and use accurately grade-appropriate conversational, general academic, and domain-specific words and phrases, including those that signal spatial and temporal relationships (e.g., After dinner that night we went looking for them). (Short Stories: Ladders A, B, C) (Poetry: Ladders A, B, C) (Nonfiction: Ladders A, B, C, D)

Cluster	Common Core State Standards in ELA-Literacy
Language, Grade 4	L.4.3 Use knowledge of language and its conventions when writing, speaking, reading, or listening. (Short Stories: Ladders A, B, C) (Poetry: Ladders A, B, C) (Nonfiction: Ladders A, B, C, D)
Language, Grade 5	L.5.1 Demonstrate command of the conventions of standard English grammar and usage when writing or speaking. (Short Stories: Ladder A)
	L.5.3 Use knowledge of language and its conventions when writing, speaking, reading, or listening. (Short Stories: Ladders A, B, C) (Poetry: Ladders A, B, C) (Nonfiction: Ladders A, B, C, D)
	L.5.6 Acquire and use accurately grade-appropriate general academic and domain-specific words and phrases, including those that signal contrast, addition, and other logical relationships (e.g., however, although, nevertheless, similarly, moreover, in addition). (Short Stories: Ladders A, C)
Literacy in History/ Social Studies, Grades 6-8	RH.6-8.1 Cite specific textual evidence to support analysis of primary and secondary sources. (Nonfiction: Ladders C, D)
	RH.6-8.2 Determine the central ideas or information of a primary or secondary source; provide an accurate summary of the source distinct from prior knowledge or opinions. (Nonfiction: Ladders C, D)
	RH.6-8.3 Identify key steps in a text's description of a process related to history/social studies (e.g., how a bill becomes law, how interest rates are raised or lowered). (Nonfiction: Ladders A, B, C, D)
	RH.6-8.5 Describe how a text presents information (e.g., sequentially, comparatively, causally). (Nonfiction: Ladders A, B)
Literacy in Science/ Technical Subjects, Grades 6-8	RST.6-8.1 Cite specific textual evidence to support analysis of science and technical texts. (Nonfiction: Ladders A, B, C, D)
	RST.6-8.2 Determine the central ideas or conclusions of a text; provide an accurate summary of the text distinct from prior knowledge or opinions. (Nonfiction: Ladders C, D)